The Brain in Pain

The Adventures of Gentle-Man

Peter Cohen

THE BRAIN IN PAIN

www.SzTheBrainInPain.com

Warning –Disclaimer

The purpose of this book is to educate and entertain. The author and/or publisher do not guarantee that anyone following these techniques, suggestions, tips, ideas, or strategies will become successful. The author and/or publisher shall have neither liability nor responsibility to anyone with respect to any loss or damage caused, or alleged to be caused, directly or indirectly by the information contained in this book.

Publisher

10-10-10 Publishing

Markham, ON

Canada

ISBN: 978-1-77277-130-5

Contents

More gentle than a summer breeze

Gentler than a landing in padded foam

Able to comfort distressed people in a single word

Look, up in the sky, it's a bird, it's a plane

No, it's Gentle-Man plunging to earth with his parachute

Gentle-Man, strange visitor from an unknown planet who came to earth with a powerful desire and ability to help his fellow mortal men. Gentle-Man, learning to swim the course of mighty rivers and bend steel in his bare hands. And who poorly disguised as Peter Cohen, mild-mannered worker for a great metropolitan practice, fights a never-ending battle for peace, love, and the Canadian way

1. He led canoe trips for five years, shot rapids, and carried canoes over anything.

2. He boxed for five years, sometimes bare-knuckle.

3. He played football for three years.

4. He did chinups and hangs from various high bridges 20 or 30 times (sick, do not do)

5. He went against advice and got straight A's from a science course at Wilfrid Laurier.

6. He took a job working with alcoholics, against advice. He stood up to their assault, bottle throwing, and other "fun."

7. He went to nursing school.

8. He asked girls for dates.

9. He stood up to a man who assaulted people.

10. He overcame agoraphobia.

11. He helped a prostitute get away from a gun-toting madman.

12. He got his PhD.

13. He held his forearm against a steaming hot kettle for 15 minutes, resulting in a huge, watery blister that took months to heal. He just smiled through it all (sick-do not do).

14. He wrote a scathing report on a wife and child abuser, who was also without conscience and stood by it.

15. He ran 32.8 miles in 6 hours and swam 5 miles in four hours. He also pressed 110 pounds over his head and bench-pressed 150 pounds.

16. He stuck with his girlfriend through thick and

thin.

17. He served in the Canadian militia.

18. He worked on a dangerous Israeli Kibbutz bordering Lebanon during a war.

19. He took part in several research studies.

20. He wrote several books.

21. He wrote several articles.

22. He saved about two dozen lives over his professional career.

23. He helped rehabilitate several people.

24. He made people more comfortable.

25. He helped some people die more comfortably.

26. He overcame generalized anxiety disorder.

27. He finished university in spite of generalized anxiety disorder.

28. He worked full time for 26 years. Dr. Stephen Gelber called this a monumental achievement. Counting school makes 40 years full time.

29. He looked after his parents for several years.

30. He looked after his mother with Alzheimer's disease 24/7 for seven years in spite of many difficulties.

31. He stood down fellow students who punched him. He did not hit them.

32. He drove himself to exhaustion on walkathons marathon runs, long distance swims and canoe trips.

33. He was resolute in danger, pain and exhaustion leading canoe trips.

34. Altogether, he had his life on the line 40-50 times and has little fear of death. He would like to die rescuing someone (sick-do not do).

35. He always looks for a chance to help someone, especially when there is some risk involved.

36. He worked on two courses while working full time at Fred Victor Mission.

37. He stayed out of institutions and off social assistance most of the time.

38. He seldom acts out with aggression in spite of the pressure of Sz.

39. He provided security and looked after violent patients several times

40. He tells people off when he gets angry enough, though most of the time he is mild-mannered.

41. He has never attacked a woman and does not punch anyone.

42. He stood in front of a charging horse to protect his girlfriend and stood in front of men who went to attack her several times.

43. He helped comfort women in frightening situations.

44. He stopped fights at Fred Victor Mission and got punched sometimes.

45. He notified police when a principal tried to murder him.

46. He worked through illness much of the time and had an ironman record at Fred Victor Mission, never missing a day and substituting for others who got sick.

47. He worked 10-12 hours at Fred Victor Mission and Grace hospital 5-6 days a week for many years.

48. He fought heavyweights and slugged toe to toe with several heavier boxers.

49. He worked long hours and studied long hours while getting his PhD.

50. He blocked and tackled guys much heavier than him at football.

51. He was the only person in the subway the morning the Armenians threatened to bomb it.

52. He kept up his strength and endurance except when too sick or too preoccupied.

53. He did 40 chest thump, arms cut away pushups every day during football person.

54. He copes with a tough disease.

55. He made something of himself in spite of a tough disease.

56. He worked while coping with anxiety.

57. He coped with the effects of extreme introversion and shyness.

58. He coped with tics and ruminations and the feeling that people could read his mind.

59. He coped with hallucinations.

60. He coped with delusions and still maintained a hold on reality.

61. He coped with distressing voices with grace.

62. He coped with severe, intractable anger with grace.

63. He loved women

64. He triumphed over sexual orientation concerns.

65. He took the bold step of marriage and looks after and cares for his wife.

66. He coped with inferiority feelings with grace.

67. He overcame depression several times.

68. He coped with physical injury with grace.

69. He coped with rejection with grace.

70. He kept his faith in people.

71. He drove himself to the point of pain and exhaustion sometimes while exercising.

72. He worked out several days while working full time.

73. He did 2-3 hours exercise each day while working full time.

74. He socialized sometimes.

75. He coped with androphobia with grace.

76. He kept his cool most of the time when legitimately provoked to anger.

77. He exercised in bad weather.

78. He wrote in spite of the handicap of Sz.

79. He coped with his girlfriend's and wife's problems with grace and empathy.

80. He can see the good in people and forgive and forget.

81. He gave up his own interests in favor of the interests of others when he felt it necessary.

82. He excelled at academics, learning to heal

people in spite of a fragile Sz he did not know about.

83. He exercised through illness.

84. He excelled at manual labour, studying, and sports, in spite of not being specifically suited to these.

85. He learned to cope with the anger and depression of his disease without resorting to suicidal behaviour. He is using these skills to help others.

86. He used the exercise high to decrease psychosis, depression, and anxiety and used his experiences to help others.

87. He worked in nursing despite homophobia.

88. He coped with loneliness.

89. He coped with a strong sex drive while still maintaining a certain morality.

90. He treated his parents well after getting treatment for his disease.

91. He overcame a smoking phobia.

92. He provided advanced nursing care to both parents and saved their lives a few times with quick thinking and good medical judgement.

93. He started back disciplined activities after getting out of the habit.

94. He took canes away from a man who used to hit people and caused a few concussions.

95. He is trained to overcome danger and pain by sports and relaxation training.

96. He went skydiving (sick-do not do).

97. His wife keeps him sharp with her powerful bare-knuckle boxing. He does not hit women.

98. He stopped a man from being attacked and pushed onto the subway tracks and got attacked himself. He did not hit anyone.

99. He stopped to help a sick and homeless man and got abused by police for it.

100. He stops to help people who are poor, sick, and downtrodden.

101. He feels guilt, a sign of goodness and maturity and is the captain, the last man down with the ship.

102. He keeps relatively fit in spite depression and the negative symptoms of Sz and several physical problems.

103. He kicked two men out of the store who were harrassing the owner. He did not attack them, but stood right in front and intimidated them with his fearlessness.

104. He did physical work in spite of painful tendonitis, arthritis, and degenerative disc disease.

105. He faced poverty and lack of food and put his wife first to the extent she would allow.

106. He cleaned high rise windows, unstrapped in to a bosun's chair and risked plunging to

107. his death.

108. He got a beating from a dominatrix and befriended her, helping her escape from an abusive man who also carried a gun.

109.   Confidence in his ability to take a punch helped him to stand up to several more

110.   bullies who harrass people and help the poor, sick, and downtrodden.

111.   He made educational history by becoming one of few people with a failing record in high school to do well enough in university to be accepted into medical school and is one of few schizophrenics accepted into medical school. Countless schizophrenics are teachers, lawyers, and engineers, but few started down a path toward medicine.

112.   He graduated from the college of hard knocks with honours.

113.   And much, much more.

114.   Because of my psychosis, this autobiography is partly an approximation of the complex and many-sided man whose adventures are recorded here.

The small boy who was afraid of everything became the man who showed himself to have little fear. The adolescent, with his life on the line many times learned that no man is exempt from mortality. The romantic activist became a pragmatic moralist who leaned that human life, his own included is forever punctuated with pain, both mental and physical.

He loved nature and the outdoors and was excellent at survival skills and outdoorsmanship, who wished he could live in previous days when there was little gadgetry and comforts to interfere with nature.

Writing was hard for him. He said that it was a truly difficult metier no matter how much you loved it, especially if you worked at it. He loved it greatly, but it was very difficult for some people.

He found that all people are alike, yet profoundly different. The book reveals the many facets of myself, , writer, canoe trip leader, lover, heroic activist and meshes work with my life.

Foreword

This book, The Brain in Pain, will show you that when you struggle with adversity, you can still bring yourself into something good. Peter Cohen will share with you that just because you are down and things look hopeless, you can still rise above it and get yourself feeling good again. Peter shows you how to modify your goals to make them more achievable and successful. For example, Peter originally wanted to be a doctor, but had great success in the field of nursing.

Peter demonstrates how you can increase your sense of courage without subjecting yourself to danger or pain by using athletic and relaxation therapy. This puts you in the enviable position of being someone of high self-esteem, having faced such adversities without subjecting yourself to the actual pain. Unfortunately, Peter learned the hard way that putting yourself in danger, pain or adversity is not necessary. With good self-care, good medical care and loving people you can thrive, grow, and lead a long, healthy, and happy life.

You may be forced to deal with feelings of inadequacy, often in a very damaging way. Peter shows how to overcome these feelings, again, without damaging/risking yourself. He explains to you that the hard way is a bad way. Peter gives tips on improving your health and well-being that he has found helpful.

The point of The Brain in Pain, aside from improving your well-being, is that you should treat others with dignity and respect, including doctors, patients, educators, students, and family members. Peter gives you pointers on how you can avoid his mistakes. Learn from Peter's knowledge today!

Raymond Aaron, New York Times Bestselling Author

Introduction

The following words will help you comprehend, a little, the phenomenon of Peter Cohen. There is first, the immensely ambitious young man, unfailingly competitive, driven by an urge to excel in anything he undertook, to be admired and looked up to, to assert his superiority by repeated example, to display for the benefit of others his strength and endurance. There is his hatred of diabetes, kidney failure, cancer, heart disease, and leukemia; his rulership over fear and pain; his proud defiance of death.

There is next, the man of many contradictions; the shy and diffident man and the incredible braggart; the tremendously warm, loving and affectionate man and the man given to tremendous hatred; the non-hero longing for hero status and sometimes achieving it; the man of action harnessed to the same chariot as the man of words and the author who impugned all cheap and easy writing, yet boiled as many pots as the next man before he was through. There is the perpetual student, the omnivorous reader and the brilliant health scientist. There is the romantic liar for whom the line between fact and fiction was thinner than a hair and who sometimes exaggerated his achievements.

There is the man driven by pride, sometimes defined as a deadly sin, but which he embraced as his personal and well-beloved demon. He was proud of his manhood, his literary and athletic skills, his staying and recuperative powers, his title, his earnings, his medical and psychological knowledge and a few other things. There is the temperamental paranoid schizophrenic, the inveterate hypochondriac and valetudinarian, who seriously contemplated suicide at times in his life, yet possessed of enormous powers of resilience and recuperation that could bring him from the brink to the peak within days, or sometimes even hours. He was a persistent worrier who wryly cautioned others against this most pernicious habit. He was plagued all his adult life with tormenting thoughts and feelings, partly the result of a highly developed imagination.

There was the muscular physique, athletic and fit, often ingratiating and impressive to some people.

He was five foot six and weighed about 155 pounds. He had a tendency to put on weight and was once up to 191 pounds. His eyes were hazel and his complexion ruddy, his head bald with salt-and-pepper hair on the sides and back. He wore a size 9 shoe.

He is said, by those who know, to have been a perfectly satisfactory lover without being a Don Juan. He formed many friendships with women, both older and younger, and considered himself to be defined by his romantic and sexual attraction towards women. He was indubitably a ladies man. There were two main loves in his life. Diane was with him for eighteen years until her cruel death. Nilani was the other main love of his life, who is married to him and they get along great. He admired courage and stoical endurance in women as in men, disliked hard backtalk, fishwifely screaming, false accusations, true accusations.

In his treatment of those he liked or loved there was often something of the chivalric; although sometimes when angered, he could be excessively cruel and abusive.

He is one of the most original health scientists Canada has produced, a powerful inventor of new techniques and ideas, such as the multi-pronged anxiety treatment, and assistance with the bioartificial kidney. He is interesting both as a professional and a man of action.

The dictionary definition of courage as steadiness in enduring danger or pain is very poor. In order to be considered to have a characteristic, it must be consistent. Giving up your life or limb is something you can only do once and so is not consistent and not therefore, a sign of courage. It is only a sign of mental illness, which is not a virtue. The doctor who caused my schizophrenia was very wrong, as you would expect from someone who turns a minor mental illness into a major mental illness. Also, the idea of competing to see who can stand the most danger and pain or who has the most "internal" strength or toughest life is similarly sick, inhuman, and barbaric.

When Peter was 15, 16, 17, and 18, he suffered from inadequacy feelings and an anti-exercise attitude that he was certain would never be resolved. These were resolved by good medical management on the part of Peter and his doctors. For Peter to put his life and limb on the line because of these feelings (as is documented in the book) turned out to be totally unnecessary. He found this out after 45 years at age 63. People should consider this when they think they must go to war and win a medal to prove themselves or listen to people like Theodore Roosevelt or George Patton. Theodore Roosevelt said "America needs a war to keep fit." George Patton said "Every man must get his" He meant that every man must serve in the military. Peter Cohen is a man of peace and is as good as any soldier.

Inadequacy feelings spread like a cancer in society because someone feeling an inadequacy feeling like shame will tend to put others down and make them feel bad. Peter wants people to build each other up by treating them with dignity and respect.

Disclaimer

The book is written by an author who himself has a medical condition. Although he is knowledgeable in some ways, the dangerous and self-damaging acts are a result and sign of mental illness. The author does not recommend these and takes no responsibility for anyone trying them.

Acknowledgements

I would like to thank first and foremost my parents, Leonard and Gretta and my sisters, Terrie and Jill for their superhuman patience in living with and helping me. I was never easy and probably never will be easy for reasons I do not pretend to understand.

Next, I would like to thank my wife, Nilani Cohen for her tremendous love and undying support. She also has superhuman patience.

I would like to thank the great Kelly Han for her inspiration, and the great Katie O'Brien for their inspiration. Both women provided life-changing experiences without realizing it.

I would like to thank Susan Williams for her friendship and inspiration.

I would like to thank Denise, Delia, Sunny, and Gail for good experiences.

I would like to thank Alice Tronson for her courage, kindness, and all around good treatment.

I would also like to thank Ken Hills for his friendship and advice.

There is great gratitude to my general physician, Dr. Philip Wong, the all-around best doctor I have ever known, who provides the best specialist care I have ever had, which is particularly remarkable because he is not a specialist.

I would like to thank Dr. George Koutsoukos for his skillful medication management and encouragement.

Gratitude to Dr. Ian Gilmore, the best specialist I have seen for excellent care and helping me cope with difficult times.

Also, gratitude to Dr. Hugh Kline, and excellent physician and my hero and idol previous to his successor, Dr. Wong.

Gratitude to the whole Diamond family for being warm and supportive.

I must thank Steve Gregory for his friendship and example as well as Valeria Smith for her support and inspiration.

Who could forget to thank military doctor, and Nobel Peace Prize Laureate Frank Sommers for his expertise, and encouragement, one of the indisputable great men of our time.

Thanks to Dr. Nisha Ravindran and Leslie Codsi for being among the best in their fields and giving great care and advice.

I would like to thank all the good people I have met for being positive influences.

Lastly, I would like to thank the good women of the world for their kindness and inspiration.

About the bad people, the less said, the better.

Most importantly. I would like to thank the great Monica Rodrigues for her inspiration and example of courage, character, and kindness that dwarfs everyone, even myself, who is very rare to be one of the few almost self-made greatness of all time.

Also I must thank the great Heidi Gabriel for her wonderful therapy, her courage, compassion, and kindness.

If there is any belief by some cruel idiots that I am not a man, or was not, if I were a child or a woman, I would get very sick and need to be transgendered and operated on as well as psychotherapied. A statement against someone's manhood after age 13 is inhuman.

Some children said, "Can Johnny come out and play?"

The mother said, "you know Johnny has no arm or legs."

They replied, "We know. We wanted to use him as third base."

In a related but true story, a lady friend of mine who was a good boxer said,

"Will you come and box with me?"

I said, "You know I don't hit women and have injured arms and legs."

She said, "I know, I wanted to use you as a heavy bag, especially since I wouldn't need gloves."

The up side to having very limited use of my arms and legs is that I cannot possibly hurt someone, even if I wanted to and I do not want to. I intensely dislike hitting people, always have, always will. Now, I have zero reason to end my life.

A Brief Overview of Mental Illness

o Schizoid Personality Disorder – Schizoid mean similar to schizophrenia. The person is disinterested in people, aloof, and very reserved about expressing feelings. Schizotypal personality is even more similar to schizophrenia and includes distorted perception.

o Schizophrenia is a disease, arguably the worst disease afflicting mankind, which consists of unrealistic and bizarre thinking, delusions, hallucinations, strong emotions such as anger, thinking difficulties, and a behavioural component.

o Somatoform Disorders – In this category. I fit also because of body image problems and hypochondriasis. My history of hypochondriasis goes back to when I was 12 and thought I was very sick and going to die. I started to read more and more about medicine, which at first aggravated the symptoms and later on resolved it. As I learned more, I realized that I could not possibly have the diseases I worried about. Also, fitness gave me the confidence that I would not get sick.

o Mood Disorders – This includes depression and bipolar affective disorder in which the person gets very high and very low. I had a patient who came to see me for depression. She described a dead end job and financial problems that got her down. I helped her find a new job and sent her to my family doctor who talked to her for an hour and put her on the SSRI antidepressant, Paxil. The new job and antidepressant made her feel better. She came back a few months later to say how well she was doing and return the job search book I gave her and express gratitude. My family doctor deserves most of the credit for putting her on Paxil.

o My depression began in grade 10 when I was assaulted by a doctor and made to feel guilty about sports and studying. In grade 11, I developed an adult type depression, felt worthless, and like I did not deserve to live. I was put on the tricyclic antidepressant, amitryptylene, which relieved the depression, but aggravated the schizophrenia. Tricyclic antidepressants must not be given to someone with schizophrenia. SSRIs and SNRIs are OK to give with schizophrenia.

o Sexual disorders include sexual orientation concerns and erectile dysfunction and are quite common.

o Substance abuse disorders include alcoholism and caffeine addiction. I am addicted to the caffeine found in tea, cocoa, and colas.

o Cognitive Disorders — I do not really fit

into this category, one of two I do not belong in. My inability to learn is caused by schizophrenia, something different. My late girlfriend suffered with Bardet-Biedl's syndrome, causing intellectual deficits, strong appetite, and a tendency to diabetes. My mother had the brain disease, Alzheimer's disease and I looked after her for seven years. She had poor memory, emotional problems, and unrealistic thinking, characteristic of a psychosis.

- Dissociative Disorders – are the second category of disorders that I do not fit into. It consists of multiple personality disorder in which someone is one person one time and someone else another time and can have any number of personalities. These are compartmentalized so that he or she does not realize he is a different personality from one time to the next. It also consists of fugues in which someone wanders off and does not remember leaving. After learning more, I found that I do have a dissociative disorder and identify with people like Ernest Hemingway, who are not necessarily good people to emulate. This is related to severe feelings of inferiority.

- Anxiety Disorders – This is the seventh of the nine categories in which I belong. Obsessive-compulsive disorder was the diagnosis for the problem in "It Takes A Woman." Introverts are the ones who tend to pick up obsessions. There are unwanted thoughts that you cannot get rid of. Phobic disorder affects everyone to some extent, but is serious if it affects day to day functioning. I have had many phobias, including agoraphobia, but have very few now. Phobias are the flip side of obsessions. Phobias cause obsessions and obsessions cause phobias. The treatment for obsessions and phobias is gradual exposure to the fear.

o My experience with post-traumatic stress disorder began in the school that I was abused in. The best case scenario for this is that I will be scarred for life. I must throw the experience in the garbage, but it requires a huge garbage can. I still get flareups of this serious condition.

o Generalized anxiety disorder was my specialty in my psychology practice. Like schizophrenia, it is partly genetic and partly situational. Unlike schizophrenia, it gets better. It feels like a big, burly lumberjack came down on your hand with all his might with a sledgehammer. Something very important to the individual is threatened. Exercise and relaxation help GAD. Exercise helps all nine psychiatric categories. It is antidepressant, antianxiety, and antipsychotic. Exercise is like a doctor – to cure sometimes, to relieve often, to comfort always.

Schizotypal Personality Disorder

My life, right from the start was tragically unhappy. I will relate my problem in terms of neuroanatomy and neurophysiology. Freud's theory is that the mind is composed of three parts – the id or primitive passions, such as hunger, thirst, sex, anger, aggression etc. The superego is the conscience, which tells us right from wrong, but sometimes in a barbaric, punishing way. The ego is the part of the mind that maintains our mental health and relatively accurate perception of reality, our will power and effective functioning, and good behaviour. The brain part that is responsible for both the superego and the id is the same and it consists of primitive parts of the brain, especially the amygdala. The hypothalamus, thalamus, pons, cingulate nucleus are also involved, though to a lesser extent. The seat of the ego is the higher mental centres such as the prefrontal cortex, the seat of will power and self-control and the frontal lobes, responsible for thinking, reasoning, and learning.

In a psychosis, the id and the superego gang up on the ego and put it out of commission, causing the symptoms of psychosis, such as schizophrenia that I described. In schizotypal personality disorder the amygdala is somewhat overactive, often the result of strong moral training combined with the naturally strong conscience that introverts show. In schizophrenia, the amygdala is much too overactive causing behavioural, thinking, and emotional difficulties. In psychopaths, people with no conscience, who can do anything they want and not feel remorse, the amygdala is much too underactive. As a consequence their primitive passions get free rein without constraints. Not only is their conscience not working, but the other function of the amygdala, the basic feelings such as fear do not work. This has been shown from magnetic resonance imaging of the brain as well as electroencephalograms. Psychopaths are a problem right from birth. I started to become a problem at about age three, when my conscience would develop. I tended to be mean, nasty, and cruel after that and a total monster after I developed schizophrenia.

In my earlier days, which were very unhappy, one of the better times was when I excelled at football. I was strong, wiry, and fast. I was also so shy that I wet the floor several times in school because I could not ask to be excused. I was labelled by the other students as meek, timid, and lazy. I hated it.

My life seemed to go relatively normally, until I was 10, when I started realizing that there was something very wrong with me. I excelled at school and sports, but was always afraid of the blocking and tackling of football, even though I liked the body contact of ball carrying. That same year, I started to increasingly fantasize about comic book characters, and unlike other boys my age I had a special need for these fantasies to come true. My MD psychotherapist told me that I had schizotypal personality disorder in those days. My thinking was so similar to schizophrenia that I thought that I had schizophrenia. I was very paranoid and believed that other children were against me and were going to rob me of my athletic abilities and make me a cripple.

In grade 6 at age 11, I became more and more disorganized due to my efforts to hide my illness and focus on my own thoughts rather than the environment. I was bright enough to get by with little study or work and I still believed, as best I could that I was not aggressive by nature and that there was something wrong with being aggressive. In truth, this only showed how maladjusted I was becoming. The degree of maladjustment that I displayed supported the theory that acting against your nature is a major cause of mental illness. However, this does not tell the whole story of mental illness. Physiological factors, neurological factors, learning factors, social factors and many more are part of the picture. For example, the main problem in schizophrenia is an excess of dopamine in the limbic system, the primitive part of the brain that governs emotion.

That year, I read a book called "The Mind In Chains," an autobiography of a schizophrenic, something like mine. This man had paranoid schizophrenia, but was not out of touch with reality, for the most part. He wrote the book to show that he was sane and was eventually discharged from the mental hospital. He believed that his history teacher, Mr. Armstrong, was controlling how everyone behaved towards him and when he realized that this was not true, he was ready to be discharged from hospital. He was given barbaric treatment, and got better in spite of it. I was also given barbaric treatment. Almost all people with a mental illness are given some form of proper treatment. The only treatments I received were abuse upon abuse upon abuse. A brutal doctor played games with my head, which is worse than no treatment at all. He entered into my delusory system and did tremendous harm. He was also the one who caused my schizophrenia. I found tremendous cruelty among family members, doctors, and educators, including psychiatrists, who are supposed to know better.

In 1965, Paul Joseph Chartier, a paranoid schizophrenic, tried to blow up the parliament buildings and everyone in it. He ended up blowing himself up in the washroom. There are jokes like "Where is Paul Joseph Chartier now that we really need him?" or "Where is Lee Harvey Oswald now that we really need him?" A psychiatrist being interviewed was asked why schizophrenics sometimes become violent and others do not. He replied that violence in schizophrenics is a matter of pushing the right buttons or the wrong buttons to look at it another way. My own story will bear this out.

At age 12, I started junior high school and was burdened with more responsibilities so that I could no longer hide my illness. Even at the beginning of the year, I wanted to see a psychiatrist because I was starting to develop every phobia available. My notes were disorganized, I could not do my homework, and was always getting detentions for neglecting one thing or another. Setting the school record for detentions, I was called down to see the vice-principal. He was sympathetic and gave me a few guidelines for organizing my work. The underlying disorder was still there, however, and I eventually broke down. I also developed hypochondriasis, which was expensive in those days because there was no universal health care.

I was hospitalized at the Hospital for Sick Children for investigation of vertigo (dizziness) which turned out to be agoraphobia, fear of open spaces. I felt that everything looked uphill and feared that I was seriously physically ill and would die soon. I said that I was dizzy because I could find no other way of describing the strange sensations I was having. These strange sensations were a part of my schizotypal personality. A theory is that these sensations are a normal part of perception, but most people do not notice it because they do not focus on it. It is form of two-dimensional vision, similar to looking at a photograph and to what happens to people in sensory deprivation experiments. People have their limbs packed so they cannot feel anything and their eyes, ears, and noses are shielded so that they developed hallucinations and left the experiment after a few days, in spite of high pay because it was very distressing.

At the hospital, after several physical tests, they took me down to see psychologists and psychiatrists. I found this so painful that I was almost in tears, although I had wanted help for years, previously. The doctors and teachers thought that my problems had started that year and I was too embarrassed to tell them that was not the case. It is very difficult to ask for help when you are young, and children are cruel and attach a stigma to mental illness. I did not have a problem asking for help when I was 15, as I became an adult, my peers did not attach a stigma to mental illness. Grades 7 and 11, I almost failed and I failed grade 12 twice, the second time much worse than the first.

When I came back to class after six months absence, the teacher had given the class a talk that I had a mental disease. A big cheer went up as I came in, shaking and trembling. They eventually got fed up with me and would call me a "chicken" and "an emergency case for 999." They hit me and kicked me and rejected me. That was more pain.

When I was 13, I could attend school more easily, though I still had a fear of halls and open spaces, and I could not take physical education classes due to agoraphobia. The other students used to make fun of me a lot. One time, the hall cleared of people, leaving a wide open space and I panicked. I broke into a run and smashed into a teacher. He said,

"Oh, do you see how dangerous that is? You go down to the office and tell them what you did."

I started off, trembling, a nervous wreck as I was every day in junior high, but the principal had seen what happened. He said,

"Go back to your room, Peter. You don't run and you won't get into any trouble."

He understood that I had just panicked from being in an open hallway.

When I was 14, I started to get over my fear of open spaces, the hard way, by entering them more and more. I became a respected football player and cross-country runner. One mean student tried to put me down by dredging up the past, but he ended up dropping out of football due to fear of body contact and I went on to star.

Nowadays, the agoraphobia would be cured in a few weeks with systematic desensitization, a painless form of behaviour therapy that was not available at that time. The doctor, who had a high reputation, believed in Freudian therapy, which has been shown to be ineffective and I found it gross and dangerous.

The therapy sessions became family therapy, in which the doctor would put me down for being passive and "acting like Hitler." He and my middle sister said that my older sister was more masculine than me because she was more aggressive. He compared me to Hitler on several other occasions and I later learned that this was not only wrong, but is a dangerous thing to do to a vulnerable person.

One of the things that helped me overcome my fear of open spaces and gave me confidence was becoming a canoe trip leader. I was hired on as staff at age 13 for showing leadership on canoe trips and being the only 13 year old who could carry a canoe. I took campers on many adventures through Algonquin Park, Haliburton, Ottawa, and Moon River. I showed tremendous drive in working on canoe trips, which illustrated my aggressive temperament. Yet I still had many of the feelings of previous years when I went back to school. I also started to get interested in girls, made awkward attempts to socialize and masturbated often. I had not real social life, and not many interests, other than thinking of girls all the time.

When I went to grade ten at age 15, it turned out to be what I regard as the happiest, healthiest year I had ever had in my life. I acted with constructiveness then, and got along well with everyone. I did all my schoolwork faithfully, attended all classes, was active in sports, over my agoraphobia completely, and was elected class president as representative on the student council. I was admired and liked by most everyone and treated everyone with respect.

I was in very good remission, and it's a darn shame it had to stop. That year was the only year I did not need medication to be a nice guy. My behaviour became even better after I completed an assertiveness training program and got rid of my anxiety. I started to do more studying, more and more exercise, felt great and showed a lot of self-discipline. If I had continued on with the self-directed behaviour therapy, I would have cured what little problems were left and excelled in high school, probably over 90%. Instead a cascade of horrifying events were triggered that I could never recover from.

The psychiatrist did not think I was doing well enough. He introduced me to a partner that I would share my therapy sessions with, an attractive 16 year old female, whom he later used to assault me with a cruel treatment that I did not want, was contra-indicated, and I would not have allowed had I known it was going to happen. The psychiatrist said with a grin,

"I think this is going to work out very well."

He later on gave me her last name, which I used to find her and start dating her, even though he had said that he did not want to play matchmaker. I think he was lying.

The doctor set up a cruel assault, using the separation of my partner's parents to make me feel guilty and making fun of my guilt saying it had sexual connotations. He started to criticize my sports and studying, and lack of socialization. He mentioned a lot of schizoid personalities who did weird things that did not apply to me. Eventually, he turned to my partner and said,

"This type of person is always looking to put himself BETTER than other people, like football."

He said in a low, punishing voice, "It's not like you, at all – studied reflections on other people."

He tried to make me feel as guilty as possible about sports and studying. He might as well have written a prescription for perphenazine at the end of the session, because it has been accurately determined that the assault was exactly what caused my schizophrenia. Also, my other problems of schizotypal personality disorder and obsessive-compulsive disorder were severely aggravated, which is what he used as an excuse for the assault.

Later, when I said that I wanted to get back to what I had in grade 10, he replied that I had not really been doing well, then, and I was looking through rose-coloured glasses because I was depressed. However, at all times, even when not depressed, I look back on grade 10 as the absolute best year of my life. He said,

"Nope, you're growing up."

In reality, I was growing downward which is what schizophrenia causes one to do. He was lying again, and was either incompetent or had things in for me. He later probably viewed my time in a concentration camp as getting what I deserved for acting like Hitler. He refused to diagnose or treat my schizophrenia or to take responsibility for causing it or the resultant behaviour. One of these behaviours was something the principal of an abusive school said was a crime and the worst possible crime. I was a destructive little punk who vandalized a school and caused tremendous damage and who hijacked an airplane and should have been shot dead. I was scum who did not deserve to live and the principal said,

"You should do something to yourself."

I knew that he was telling me to kill myself.. The doctor said I was lucky to have had the opportunity to be in an abusive school and just did not make anything of the opportunity. He also said later that the idiotic voices of my relative, guidance counsellor, and principal were probably right because he did not realize that they were hallucinations. No hallucination is right or worth being guided by. He said earlier that psychiatry could do great harm even with a highly skilled practitioner. This was an instance just like that. The doctor brought about wonderful memories.

Journey Into Madness – Schizophrenia

The summer after I was assaulted, I went to camp as a tripper, but was no longer any good. I had nothing of my usual enthusiasm and was uncharacteristically irresponsible in leading canoe trips. This is in keeping with my idea that schizophrenia causes one to grow down rather than up. When I came back after the summer, I could not concentrate on school and was starting to act like descriptions of schizophrenics. I mentioned this to the doctor, but as usual he just discounted it and told my parents and I that I was just not motivated. Lack of motivation is very unusual for me. The doctor should have been sued for malpractice, but I only found out a few years ago that he caused my schizophrenia. He caused everything bad that happened to me and everything bad that I had done. He had a lot of guilt on his hands, but I was the one with the sense of responsibility and he just laughed it all off, which is puerile. I intensely dislike him now that I have found out what he did to me.

The girl that the doctor used in his assault, and who was my partner in therapy, became my first friend who was a girl. We dated once in 1968 and several times in 1969. We would walk hand in hand and arm in arm. Our first kiss occurred in a field with railway tracks just behind her house. We were behind a fence a few houses away from her house. I faced her and said,

"I have something to say to you."

I gently, but firmly put my hands on her shoulders and leaned closer to her. She must have known what was coming.

"Say it." she said

I put my lips closer and closer to hers and finally kissed her full on the lips. I tasted her lips, like wine, and we kissed for a few moments. She then hugged me with her powerful arms and said a prolonged, "Oh."

It was the first kiss for both of us. I don't know how she felt, but I will remember it forever. We dated a few more times and eventually she told me that we would have to part because I loved her and she did not feel the same for me. She said that I was getting too dependent on her. In fact, my dependence was a sign of my developing schizophrenia. By rejecting me for it, she actually aggravated it. I never became independent either emotionally or financially as a result of the schizophrenia. However, we must play the hand we are dealt and the director of a psychotherapy institute said that I did a tremendous amount with one of the worst set of cards anyone could be dealt.

I expressed anger to my friend at our last conversation. In retrospect, I believe she was very courageous in the way she expressed her feelings towards me, an example of how courageous she had been all her life. She was very feminine and emotionally satisfying. She liked to describe herself as a coward. I wish I could tell her how courageous she had been. It was not her fault that I became sick after the assault by our doctor.

After our relationship ended, I started to show definite signs of schizophrenia and became very weird. I forced myself to socialize even though I was not truly interested in people. I also exercised little and could do no schoolwork. My reading ability was poor and I had great difficulty focusing on what teachers were saying. Schizophrenia usually comes along with a learning disability, which I had all through my teen years and later became permanent in nursing school.. I did not reach my potential even though my IQ is in the top 6% of the population. I did very well in university (a) because of a strong aggressive drive to excel and (b) because my medication agreed with me so very well.

In grade 10, I was very puritanical about smoking, drinking, drugs, and sex and was at odds with my family about sports and these puritanical beliefs. This conflict added to the damage done by my doctor's assault. It is a non-issue now as most of the family gets along well, and my family was then and is now, great. I am the black sheep of the family. My mother said that I was "just a little kid" in grade 10, probably because she did not like my Puritan endeavours, but in reality, I acted more maturely then, than ever before or ever after. Schizophrenia makes one mean and acting childishly, even babyish. I was a true man before I developed schizophrenia. It also saps your courage, as any illness will. Also, most of the mean criticisms by people, such as my principal would not have come about if I had not developed schizophrenia.

Halfway through grade 11, I started to get aggressive with the girls at school and the family. I started to develop a delusion of grandeur that I was the only perfect person in the world and I must correct everyone else's faults. I started to act in ways that I thought were opposite to my doctor's assault because I knew it was bad. It was an anti-exercise philosophy that caused my schizophrenia, but unfortunately exercise will not cure it. It only ameliorates it. One behaviour of schizophrenia, fighting, occurred when I was in very good condition, but because it was caused by schizophrenia, therefore it was caused by an anti-exercise philosophy. I started to play with locks of girls' hair and take things and give it back to them. The girls complained and I was sent down to the school psychologist who told me to stop this abusive behaviour. I agreed. He phoned my doctor and told him that I had schizophrenia and must be put on medication as soon as possible. This made my doctor angry and he said that I could not possibly have schizophrenia because I was not weird. He felt badly because the problems I had been having were caused by his earlier assault.

This was the behaviour that my MD psychotherapist said the psychiatrist missed the diagnosis of schizophrenia. Most parents call an ambulance or take their children to the hospital when their children have their first episode psychosis like that. My mother, instead kicked me and gave me a great deal of abuse and further voiced her contempt of me. My sister said, "Throw him out in the rain!" She used to bait me to get abusive even when I was not inclined to do anything wrong. For example she would tell me that I did not have the guts to tell her off and then cry when I told her off. She later confessed that she was glad to see me suffer like that, even though she did not like the abuse. Anyway, that was the extent of the treatment I got. My family loved to throw shame and guilt at me which will be discussed later.

It turned out the school psychologist's diagnosis of Sz was 100% correct, and it was caused by the assault by my doctor the previous year. This is termed iatrogenic schizophrenia. I was made to act against my introverted nature and this caused anxiety and stress, causing the hippocampus and amygdala in the brain to be saturated with cortisol and adrenaline, adding methyl and amine groups to histone proteins in the brain, making a dopamine factory there. From then on, I was very sick all the time and was never the same again. I developed a conscience-related depression, which adults get, but rarely adolescents. The delusions of reference, delusions of grandeur, and delusions of persecution were replaced by a feeling that I did not deserve to live. My suicidal ideation made me very anxious.

I was put on amitryptylene, a tricyclic antidepressant that made my schizophrenia much worse because these drugs act by increasing catecholamines in the brain, including dopamine. This caused worsening delusions and hallucinations. I told the doctor that I felt like I was on an LSD trip, even though I had never done illegal drugs in my life. He just laughed and asked,

"Have you been doing LSD?"

I felt like newscasts were directed at me and public speakers were talking at me. These are called "delusions of reference." I felt that people could read my mind which was very distressing. This continued until I was put on steady neuroleptic medication. I was also bothered by twitching of my facial muscles, called tics, and internal monologues, called ruminations. People, by reading my tics and ruminations, sometimes felt they could read my mind. However, my ruminations did not reflect what was really going on in my mind. Sz is treated with the same medications as Gilles de la Tourrette's syndrome and is suspected to have a related cause. Tourrette's syndrome is a tic disease in which the person says exactly what he does not want to say. If he is in front of someone he will deliver a slur to that person's race or religion and, if the person is ignorant enough, he will not know that it does not represent the person and that he cannot help it. This might be why my principal hated me so much and wanted to murder me.

The treatment that I got was for the doctor to show remorse for his assault, antidepressants, and increased exercise. The latter was more helpful. The remorse for his assault just pushed the buttons to give me an obsessive hatred. I passed grade 11 and became a tripper again. I was no longer much good at it and was thinking about my obsessive hatred.

I came back from the summer thinking I was doing very well and getting a B average in school. My obsessive hatred turned into a criminal act and because of circumstances and poor treatment I went badly and progressively downhill. The doctor claimed I was going through a Nazi stage caused by exercise.

This angered my MD psychotherapist when I told him about the incident many years later. He said the psychiatrist did not know what the hell he was talking about. Bigots like the Nazis, Adolf Hitler, and Hermann Goering were pathological personalities, no conscience and grandiosity and evil. He told me I had no reason to feel guilty because I had acted as any mentally ill person would. He told me that the fault lay with the psychiatrist for missing the obvious diagnosis and not giving me medication. Even later, if I did not get my medication, I would have difficulty controlling myself. One of my coping mechanisms is to turn the anger in on myself. This is not good, but I prefer it. I read that schizophrenics treated with psychotherapy alone went downhill more rapidly than patients who got no therapy, who also went badly downhill.

The doctor gave me the worst possible treatment

for Sz and the place I was the next year just gave me horrible abuse which is the worst thing that can be done for mental illness and was totally inhumane and barbaric.

All the modern day mental health professionals in my adult life said that I was not criminally responsible.

I failed grade 12 and my doctor suggested that I go to a private school. He mistakenly thought that my parents had money. He was dead wrong because I ended up helping to support my parents and they did not leave me a penny after they died. Also, sending someone to another school does no good whatsoever because the person just takes his problems to another school.

The next year was a mistake. It ws the most hellish, nightmarish year I had ever experienced in my life. The principal was a bigoted Quaker who did not understand his religion, did not believe in it and did not practice it. It is always the most bigoted people who know the least about their own religion. The only thing he ever thought about was punishing me, living in the past. He fought to get me to come to his school because it presented a unique opportunity to find a vulnerable man against whom he could express his hatred and bigotry. He had never seen this before. All other students just laughed his nonsense off. He was a bully and people bully others because they perceive vulnerability. He encouraged other students to bully me and punch me because violence was against his religion. My MD psychotherapist said that this fellow was a pathological personality and a characteristic of this is they like to manipulate others to do their violence for them He once found another student beating me up and gave him a pat on the back and told him to keep it up.

"He'll listen to you as well as to me," he said.

The students who beat me up physically were being kind to me compared to the principal. The police and decent people everywhere all hated him. Mental health professionals said,

"This man disgusts me."

I was turned off the Quaker religion for a long time until out of curiosity I started to read about the Quaker religion. He broke every rule of the Quaker religion. I have become a Jewish Quaker and neither I nor any of my fellow Quakers are anything like this bigot. We are real Quakers in contrast to him. I need that now just like I needed proper treatment. I got neither back then.

My principal was also breaking the law by counselling me to commit suicide, especially since he knew that I was vulnerable. When I contacted the police, they said he should be locked up and have the key thrown away. They also said that in constantly telling me I did not deserve to live, he was being hypocritical and committing violence. He did not care that I almost died the next year due partly to an obsessive-compulsive disorder that he caused. A wise doctor told me to throw the nonsense of the principal in the garbage and the nonsense of the head of guidance in the garbage and any other nonsense that came along. Some things require a massive garbage can. The more he perceived vulnerability, the more abusive he became. One time when someone vandalized the school and flooded the meeting room with a fire hose causing massive damage to the whole building, he gave a speech that had nothing to do with someone vandalizing his school. He began by saying,

"There is not one person, student or staff who cannot live up to his dreams at this school. Maybe you'll see why we have rules against waterbombing and water bombing is cowardly and this crime is cowardly. That person who stole, is that what you want to be for the rest of your life, a thief? Let's stick together on this dastardly act. Then he pointed at the floor and emphasized the word, hit. To HIT us with this crime."

Waterbombing did not go on at the school. He had been alluding to boxing when he talked about waterbombing. He talked about the law the way Adolf Hitler talked about the law. Adolf Hitler said that Germany's freedom was made up of laws. He then broke the law by murdering 11 million people and starting WWII. My principal said the same thing and then broke the law, as I described. Hitler and this guy used to manipulate laws and religion for their own purpose.

I failed grade 12 again, failing even worse than the year before, only passing two subjects, neither one more than 50% I failed due to a worsening schizophrenia, caused by the abuse from the principal and was bothered with his voice whenever I did not feel good, which at one time became frequent. When I jumped in front of the subway at age 34, I thought how happy it would make this principal. I was relieved to get away from this bigot.

I spent the summer in Israel, recovering from the abuse given by the principal. Not one good thing came out of the concentration camp. A great deal of bad things came out of it, some of which showed up later. Israel was a great place filled with a peaceful bunch of people, who did not like me because they could somehow tell that I had a psychiatric history, probably from my tics and ruminations. I enjoyed working on the farm bordering Lebanon, called a Kibbutz, the joy of travelling, and climbing Mount Masada. After I was put on medication, I did not enjoy travelling and could hardly fly, which is something that did not bother me back then.

I was let forward into grade 13 and eventually did very well in public school because I was concentrating on exercise. It was almost, but not quite, like being in grade 10 again. A lot of the girls found me interesting because of my exploits in Israel and football, and daredevil stunts. I enjoyed this adoration and still feel love and gratitude to the girls who were so kind and understanding and accepting. They touched my heart and I would never do anything to upset them. Some said that I deserved a medal, which eventually came in several different ways.

I would have done much better if the head of guidance, who was a horrible bully, had not called me down to the office and told me that I had no chance of passing grade 13. If he had proper qualifications or intentions he would have known that you never say that to someone as it may turn into a self-fulfilling prophecy. He did not care. He purported to be "very concerned about me." In reality, he only wanted to try to bully me back into the concentration camp to face certain failure and certain death because of his hatred for me which he later admitted to. I had had emotional problems and they might come back, he said in his sing-song voice. I would just get into "all kinds of trouble" in spite of the fact that I had never been a troublemaker. The problems that I had had were the result of schizophrenia and he essentially wanted to bar me from the public education system because of schizophrenia. That is cruel discrimination and an unprofessional and immoral show of hatred, which amounted to an abuse of power. It was like a bigoted immigration officer trying to send a Jew back to Nazi Germany after he escaped. He even lied through his teeth, saying that I had passed in the concentration camp, wouldn't I go to where I passed. He had my marks in front of him and could see that I had failed. He was out of touch with reality.

By the time I got to the private school, much of the brain damage had already been done, but what the principal did to me was much worse than the beatings I got from my fellow students. It was worse than caning me for several hours each day and beating me over the head with a thick cane and causing brain damage. A SPECT scan of the brain showed massive brain damage and he had a part in it. Also, he justified his abuse saying that it prevented me from doing anything wrong. However, if I had even the slightest thought of doing anything wrong, his abuse would have brought it to fruition. The experience at the private school was permanently damaging and I certainly did not need more damage.

I proved that the guidance counsellor was wrong by passing grade 13 with a 62% and later on getting accepted at Ross University medical school, all of which he said I could not do. Also, he said that he wanted to prevent me from getting hurt. That was absurd, because his abuse was very hurtful. Rejection from medical school or even failing school as I did in the concentration camp could not be nearly as hurtful as his cruel abuse. His theory of not trying anything for fear of getting hurt was the ultimate in cowardice as was picking on a vulnerable student. I would have failed permanently if I had listened to this jerk.

As Susan Jeffers said,

"You're not a failure because you didn't make it. You're a success for having tried."

University

I took correspondence courses during my year off and worked as a reporter for the Globe and Mail while I applied to universities. It is a good thing that I worked before going to university and that I won a big scholarship at university because my parents did not have the money to send me to university.

I was in remission all during my undergraduate years in Waterloo because I was taking neuroleptic medication. The neuroleptic that I was on was perphenazine, the second neuroleptic to come on the market after chlorpromazine. My response to perphenazine was dramatic and miraculous, a major cause of good things in my life and I am very grateful for it, eternally grateful, in fact.

It happened with some difficulty. I had been working on a tobacco farm for a few months with long hours of strenuous labour that I enjoyed. I did not get much sleep. After the job ended, I came back feeling guilty about helping people to smoke and very crazy. I started throwing out ashtrays, glasses, dishes, and anything that remotely resembled an ashtray. It was a culmination of needing medication for four and one half years. My great sister (both are great) knew I was sick and called the doctor who put me in the psychiatric ward at North York General. I should have been sent there four years earlier instead of the abusive road I was sent on, but all's well that ends well. The attending doctor, an excellent man kept me in for two months. I was nervous about being there because I thought they might change me for the worse. Instead they changed me for the better. I was on heavy medication at first and was sleeping for 22 hours a day for a while. This high dosage was eventually reduced and I could get up and move around. I was discharged on a low dose of trifluoperazine, which was later changed to perphenazine because trifluoperazine causes restlessness.

As I said, the perphenazine was a major factor in my success. It reduced my level of anger and made me feel good. It acted on all three aspects of Sz. It took away the cognitive deficit that caused a learning disability. It took away the affective component (mostly anger) and made conative (behavioural) symptoms exceedingly unlikely. It stopped my delusions of grandeur, persecution and reference. I still had auditory hallucinations, which went away when I finished first year university with 91%. My doctor said that I grew out of the Nazi stage as a result of the therapy I received at North York General. The Nazi stage lasted 4 and a half years while I was undiagnosed and untreated. In reality, Sz had been my problem all along. North York General just plunked me in a bed and pumped me full of drugs. I got the treatment I had needed for four and a half years. I doubt that there is a such thing as a temperament that needs something to hate as I am only full of love. I might have called this book what Hitler wanted to call Mein Kampf, "Four and a half years Against Lies, Stupidity, and Cowardice." When I went off my medication, to my doctor's credit, he balled me out for not taking my medication and told me that if I did not take it, he would put me in a hospital and they would force me to take my medication. He gave my parents strict orders to apply Toughlove – they were to kick me out at the slightest sign of belligerence or not taking my medication. Dr. Henry Rosenblatt said that 80% of schizophrenics cannot live with their families. For 3 years, I should not have lived with my family and welcomed being away. The doctor went to his grave never knowing that I had schizophrenia or that he caused it. One of the points of this work, besides challenging the stigma of mental illness is that schizophrenics can be likeable people, also loveable to some people. We are not the heinous, weird people, similar to psychopaths that my psychiatrist made us out to be Most of us are warm, sensitive, caring and in one way or another, productive. We are especially nice when we get our medication. A nurse at CAMH said, later on,

"You seem like a really nice guy. I don't thing you were responsible for the things you said you did."

She was right.

In university, I worked 16 hours a day, 7 days a week to get the high marks I needed for med school, graduate school or nursing school. I was successful in learning at nursing school and graduate school. One of the things I did not like about university was the constant work to get very high marks and no other interests. I did 10-20 minutes of exercise each day for strength and endurance, but if I had done it more scientifically, I would have felt better. Also, if I had done the relaxation therapy that later cured an anxiety disorder, I would have felt better.

The World of Work

When I graduated, I could not find a job and had even worse anxiety and had even worse anxiety than I had in university because I knew that my parents could not support me. I had to go to a rehabilitation workshop at minimum wage and take relaxation therapy for the anxiety. I worked full time in the workshop and part time at a higher paying job to pay the bills. The workshop, because it was rehabilitation gave me time off to take relaxation therapy.

Eventually, after two months, it worked big time. However, the weekend before it worked, I took 25 five mg. Aspirins because the brilliant psychiatrist who caused my schizophrenia, told me that there was nothing could be done about anxiety and I would have to get used to it. I thought he might be right and an intolerable situation combined with no hope of improvement is the recipe for suicide. I'm glad I lived and have no ill effects from the aspirin because many people suffer damage from that much aspirin. I felt better after I got rid of the side effects of the aspirin and the anxiety never came back in the same way. When I found my first real full time job, my anxiety level went down even more. I later learned that relaxation is a bravery-enhancing technique and can make you absolutely fearless as has been shown by many people many times. If I were a military commander, I would give my troops relaxation training and the result would be fearless troops. I had a better sense of courage after the relaxation training than when I had the anxiety disorder, in spite of the kind words of the abnormal psychology textbook.

My first job was at the Fred Victor Mission, working as a nursing attendant in a home for older men.

While working at the mission, the government ruled that my job would have to be filled by a registered nurse. Several men died because the attendant on duty did not have enough knowledge to deal with emergencies. We were on duty totally alone, in charge of 67 men, many being critically ill and any emergency could be thrown at you at any time, especially medical emergencies. One time a man went into heart failure and the Chinese doctor helped me get him to the hospital. They could develop life-threatening pneumonias, strokes, heart attacks, and many other emergencies.

After working at the Fred Victor Mission for several years, I was accepted into nursing school where you needed at least 80% just to have a chance to get in. I worked part time two days a week while going to school full time. I was given advance standing due to my previous work and courses, including premed, PSW, and auditing the paramedic course. I went to nursing school with the idea that I would go back to my old job once I graduated. I liked studying the nursing subjects and learning to do better nursing care and enjoyed being one of only four males in a female-dominated class of 136 students. The women were beautiful and caring. I also enjoyed the reduced workload of only having to work 12-14 hours a day, five days a week, and only 4-6 hours on weekends. I was used as a tutor for other students because of my previous experience. I did well in my first two years, but in my third year after a small amount of anxiety with some family problems, I developed a learning disability from which I have never recovered. This occurred from brain damage to a brain already damaged by schizophrenia, much in the way schizophrenia is caused, as I described.

I was very disappointed at not being able to finish nursing school, but even more disappointing was that I was accepted at Ross University medical school, but could not attend it for the same reason. This was most unfortunate and frustrating because the school said that anyone with a GPA of 2.9 or higher had always completed the course. I had a 3.43. Unable to finish nursing school, I went back into the world of work and tried to find a diagnosis and treatment for my learning disability. Doctors came up with a different diagnosis for each one I saw. One doctor even referred me to a hooker. It was a pleasant experience but it did not help me learn better and is a bad habit. I should have sued that doctor as I could have sued many other doctors. Dr. G. in 1987, who was an excellent psychiatrist told me that the learning disability was most likely due to schizophrenia. It is a disorder of memory and attention, among other things and affects the hippocampus and amygdala, the seat of the limbic system that also governs memory, attention, and emotion. Most doctors know it as a cognitive deficit. They tend not to understand learning disability that accompanies schizophrenia. In 2010, while watching a program put on by David Suzuki, featuring a psychiatrist, Norman Doidge, an expert on neuroplasticity, which is changing the brain through experience, I learned that the treatment for the learning disability was discovered in 2009 by Dr. Sophia Vinagradov, conducting research protocols in San Francisco, California. It is not well known that this learning disability is the major source of pensions in North America, and if a schizophrenic does not have this disability, there is no justification for a pension. Someone who lives with his parents and double dips with a pension is particularly egregious. Many people get away with it. Some are right wingers who disapprove of social programs, but are eager to cheat the system when they get the chance.

In early 2014, experiments with this treatment came to Toronto, but I did not qualify for the experiment because I have a comorbidity of major depressive disorder and am too old by six years.

After nursing school, I worked in rehabilitation nursing at St. John's Hospital for a few years, but wanted to stop when my nursing care went downhill because of the obsessive disorder described later. I greatly enjoyed working at St. John's until age 29, when my obsessive disorder developed.

I left my job at St. John's after finding a job as a porter at Grace Hospital that involved little nursing care. I left St. John's on a Friday and started Grace on the Monday after that weekend, April 4, 1984. I loved the job and thrived there. Incidentally, the pay was excellent, but I did not know that when I took the job. I eventually wound up working six days a week, 10 hours a day. I did not mind as I was grateful to have a job. Also, I had worked longer hours many other times in my life so this was still a break. This shows the importance of temperament in adjustment. One of the signs of aggressiveness is working very hard. Aggressive people and anyone can show good adjustment, if shown how. The therapist shows how and the patient does the work. I have always thrived on hard work and discipline and my aggressive temperament is one of the reasons I could work full time. Dr. Henry R. told me in 1987 that 90% of schizophrenics cannot work and the ones who can only work volunteer or part time. New medications have only improved the picture a little, according to Dr. E. Fuller Torrey. Some doctors have practices with most of their schizophrenic patients working full time, but these practices are not representative. Also, people with drug-induced psychoses are often misdiagnosed as schizophrenics. It is extremely rare for someone with schizophrenia to get a doctorate, but some do as I did. Most doctors do not believe I have a doctorate. I also met Diane soon after starting Grace Hospital. I moved in with her after six months, but still kept up my responsibilities to my parents and was with Diane until her cruel death in June of 2001.

Breakdown

I continued to cook for and help my parents part time as I had been doing all along. I left Grace Hospital after a few years and worked as a courier full time for the Messengers until April of 1987. All of a sudden, the perphenazine, my miracle drug stopped working and I got very angry, my violent past made me feel very guilty and I started to hear tormenting voices that put me into a rage. I had not seen Dr. G. for a year, but he agreed it was an emergency and saw me immediately. He listened to my tale of woe and said that I had a biochemical imbalance, which he later told me was schizophrenia and should not feel guilty. He told me he could put me back into remission with pimozide, usually used to treat Gilles de la Tourrette's syndrome. He had the right general idea and said that the guilt would go away when the anger went away and antidepressants were contra-indicated. Unfortunately, in spite of the good response and low side effect profile that most patients on pimozide had, it did not agree with me and it aggravated my psychosis, did not help the anger and caused the worst akathisia (restlessness) than from any other drug I had ever taken. Work was agonizing. I stayed on it for several weeks, but fearing that I was going to hurt someone, and listening to the counsel of my principal's voice (I was delighted to read that he died the previous year), I jumped onto the subway tracks in front of an oncoming train. Someone yelled,

"You there, stop that!"

When I did not move, he pulled the cutoff switch and the train came to a halt a few feet from where I was standing. The conductor, who was also a firefighter, restored the power, brought me onto the train and called an ambulance. They took me to a Toronto hospital where the treatment was quite incompetent and barbaric. The doctor in charge of my case was an intern with no training or interest in psychiatry. He was very immature, mean, and arrogant. He would not listen to me or the much more skilled, trained, and highly experienced Dr. G. He thought he knew everything because he was an MD. I told him that I was having a flareup of my schizophrenia and needed neuroleptic therapy. He said,

"You do not present as a schizophrenic. You present with a picture of a deep-seated depression. He later confessed that he just assumed that I was depressed because he was told that I had jumped in front of the subway. He never talked to me or did an assessment, which is probably because he did not know how. The staff psychiatrist, who was supposed to be supervising the intern, also never saw me and just said yes to all the idiotic ideas of the intern.

The intern decided to treat me with amitryptylene, the very same tricyclic antidepressant that had severely aggravated my schizophrenia when I first showed signs of it at age 16. I asked the intern not to give me the drug and he said,

"I know you think it is the wrong treatment, but I'm the doctor and I know best."

The staff man said yes to this idiotic idea as he said yes to the idiotic idea of taking me off neuroleptics, which was abandoned when I proceeded to beat myself to death, as they had tried to make sure there was nothing available to suicide on.

As each day passed, I got sicker. I was

hallucinating profusely, seeing the face of my principal laughing at me and flying at me. I got the delusion that I was Hitler and felt pathetically bad, much worse than when I came in. One nurse, suspecting that the treatment was wrong, got an order for chlorpromazine to help me, but could not take me off the antidepressants because she was not an MD. She proved to be very courageous. She would always put her face close to mine when she talked to me. That made me feel good because it showed that she was not afraid of me. She was also attractive, but I only vaguely cared about it at the time. Her name was Valerie. Another nurse, Lynn was very good. The nurses were generally nice, but tended not to like me because I was actively psychotic at the time. When Diane brought me a shirt and said,

"I spoil him."

A nurse said, "Someone did."

This showed that they did not know me because I was acting very atypically. Finally, after six days on amitryptelene, I woke up in a rage and started banging my head against the wall. I told the night nurse that I was losing control of myself. She said,

"Don't worry. We'll put you in restraints."

I voluntarily let the orderly chain all my four limbs to the bed. It is a hellish experience that I would not wish on anyone. The intern came in the next morning and said,

"We're cutting your antidepressants by half." I said, "I guarantee, I'm not depressed."

He exclaimed, "Then how come you jumped in front of the subway?"

I said emphatically, "To get rid of my anger."

He told me, OK, that he would relent and stop the antidepressants. Seeing some light at the end of the tunnel, and helped by chlorpromazine, I stopped acting on my psychotic thoughts and was soon discharged from the hospital. I felt better when the pimozide was stopped and the perphenazine was given four times a day, instead of all at once at night. Once the pimozide was stopped, the restlessness went away. Once the perphenazine was given 4 times a day I had an even flow of it in my bloodstream and the anger subsided a great deal. The intern did not know or care that he was wrong and said as a parting shot,

"If you have a problem, don't go running to Dr. G. for more drugs, handle it on your own."

That is like telling a cancer patient that if his cancer comes back he shouldn't go running to the doctor for more chemotherapy, he should handle it on his own. Dr. G. was horrified that they would put an intern totally in charge of someone's care with no supervision. He said that the intern sounded very immature and arrogant and should not be a doctor. He put me on a drug that Dr. Gilmore told him was bad. I needed a top notch specialist like the one at North York General, but I did not get it until I was discharged back into Dr. G.'s care. He said to continue taking the perphenazine four times a day and if I had another flareup, he would just increase the perphenazine. Later, while working at a stockbroking house, it was increased from 4 mg. Four times a day to 6 mg four times a day. I started exercising more and more and found that I got an exercise high when I did an hour or more of aerobic exercise. It is anti-anxiety, anti-depressant, and anti-psychotic. When I was doing two and a half to three hours of exercise a day, I felt great. Those were very happy times.

This stopped when I got tired of working at an immoral stockbroker's job and went to work in a psychiatric home for a year. Because of my seniority, I did much overtime, about 60 hours a week and no longer had time for long periods of exercise. I was somewhat ill-suited to the job as it was smoke-filled with 15 of the 16 residents being heavy smokers and in order to talk to them you had to breath in smoke. Also, there was much unstructured talking that was not my strong suit.

After that, I went to work for a nursing registry called Comcare and did an hour of exercise a day, usually running. I felt good until 1989, when, while listening to a football game one night, I got worked up and could not sleep, triggering another flareup. I increased the perphenazine to 8 mg and went to North York General and told them that I had been good for 15 years and they had helped me and could they please help me again? The intern did a thorough assessment and I could tell that he had vast quantities of medical knowledge, but did not know how to use it well. He concluded,

"Have you ever been treated for depression?"

I replied that I had been treated for depression but I had not been depressed. They had the wrong diagnosis. He sent in the psychiatry intern who was excellent and empathetic and caring. Her name was Dr. S. and I sent her a thank you note for saving my life after I got out. She admitted me after consulting with the staff psychiatrist. He also thought I was depressed, but was smart and phoned Dr. G. and listened to him when he was told that I was having a flareup of my schizophrenia. I was markedly improved in four days and he was very proud. He gradually lowered my perphenazine and I was discharged without incident two weeks later, thanks to his wisdom.

I went back to work for Comcare and continued to exercise. Dr. G. experimented with haloperidol periodically when perphenazine did not work well enough. If I took it every other day 5 mg, the restlessness would not take hold because the side effects of haloperidol do not start until a second straight day.

I continued to work until I was absolutely too sick and my in-laws had to help me support Diane. I did not get definitive relief until Dr.G. had heard enough of my psychosis and gave me six weeks of free samples of risperidone in August, 1995. I took medication so that I could work and worked so that I could pay for the expensive medication. I later joined the Trillium drug program to help pay for my medication. I am grateful to one of our best premiers, Bob Rae for starting it.

Graduate School

In 1991, I was accepted into a PhD program, after much anxiety because PhD programs are harder to get into than medical school. I worked in market research and medical editing to support Diane while I went to grad school. I worked six hours a day six days a week and studied 4-6 hours a day. The learning disability/cognitive deficit did not affect my coursework because evaluation was based on writing – essays and theses. I designed a program, after getting information from University of Toronto medical school, that paralleled the medical course. The professor could evaluate me because he was a quadruple doctor and an RN. On August 5, 1999, I was awarded my PhD. It felt especially good because it required a great deal of high level work and creativity. I immediately stopped market research and opened up a practice of psychology. I found it was difficult to constantly market myself but I managed to eke out a living until I went on Canada Pension Plan when my father, my mother's previous caregiver, died on Friday, December 13, 2002. I had to look after my mother 24 hours a day, 7 days a week and could do no exercise. I put on so much weight that I became pre-diabetic with a blood sugar of 6.1. After six years of looking after my mother and getting up to 191 pounds, the doctor said that if I did not get help looking after my mother, I would die. We got a little bit of help in and I lost 51 pounds over the next year.

I did all the nursing care for my mother and my experience in nursing came in handy. I would patch up my mother when she would injure herself and comfort her when she would hallucinate. She also became very paranoid and did everything to me with her Alzheimer's disease that I did to her with my schizophrenia. My mother would often walk over to my bed, wanting sex, and pee on my bed. I would try to explain to her that I was her son and did not want to commit incest, which she accepted. She could be very sweet at times and would want me to take her hand. I read that it was a potent technique for comforting the confused.

After my mother died of a perforated bowel on October 3, 2009, I had to stay on CPP because for many reasons I could not work, anymore for about 1 and a half years. My mother was in stage 4 when she died, which is the stage before coma and death. She became so confused that I had to feed her. She forgot how to eat. I also had to clean her up quite often. A few months before she died, I had to move into her room because she broke her hip and would fall or have tremendous pain when she tried to take a step I would awake when she got up to use the washroom and encourage her to use the commode. She would ask,

"Why can't I just use the washroom."

I would say, "Take a step and you'll find out why."

She had tremendous pain when she would try to take one step. On month before she died, I had a nervous breakdown and the doctor decided to put her in a home. She died waiting for placement.

A Celebration of the Greatest Beings Ever To Grace The Planet (women) An Existentialist View

Women are the greatest thing ever to grace the planet. For one thing, they are all extremely beautiful and can lift someone out of a depression or bad mood just by being looked at. They are called the fair sex for good reason. They are a noble subset of a potentially noble mankind and the best example of it. Men are good, but women are great.

Women are kinder, gentler, and nicer than most men, and have more compassion. As a result of this, they are better at the helping professions, such as medicine, law, nursing, and psychology. They also have superior intelligence because the genes for intelligence are coupled with the genes for attractiveness. They have more patience and as a result are better at everything they do, especially nonphysical pursuits. In spite of this, women, such as Diana Nyad, Vicki Keith, and Angela Kondrak have set records in marathon swimming, which requires strength and endurance as well as great courage.

Women have made great contributions to all aspects of human endeavour and would have made greater contributions if chauvinists had not put them in a subversive role. Women are also more accepting of multi-faceted roles such as homemakers, housewives, mothers, and wage earners.

They play a tremendously important biological role in doing the difficult part of reproduction. The courageously and stoically put up with the danger and pain of carrying and bearing children.

These roles are dwarfed by what their very existence can do for mankind. They help nurture and comfort all of mankind, including other women, but they especially boost the morale, motivation, and well-being of men. This shows an example of what Paul Tillich called "The courage to be." Women are the very reason for men's existence, not only from a biological standpoint, but from a motivational standpoint. One of a man's main goals is to earn the respect and admiration of women. Without women, little would get done by anyone.

A women can make a man feel good and raise his spirits. The chiropractic assistant shows great compassion by waving to me as I walk by the office. She is so strong that she can lift up a 165 pound man with just a little wave of her hand. They lift our spirits by talking to us and their kind words. My wife is outstandingly beautiful and does everything for me, including things I tend to neglect. I call her Saint Nilani.

When a woman enters into a relationship with a man, it makes both the man and woman feel good. It is a win-win situation. It makes the man feel more masculine and the woman feel more feminine. This is also true of a physical sexual relationship. However, any relationship between a man and a woman, even the remotest non physical kind, or even from a distance, I would consider a sexual relationship. One treats the opposite sex different from the same sex.

Even priests and monks, who are celibate, need women. Also, men of same-sex orientation can appreciate women greatly, just not in the same way that I do. There is nothing wrong with same-sex preference. They are also an important part of society.

I define courage as a will to extend yourself to do something useful. All people, but especially women are doing something useful just by living. If we do not have courage, we lose the will to live and subsequently die. Living is hard and dying is easy. I say this from the point of view of a man who has faced death between 40 and 50 times. If I had died it would have been the simplest and easiest thing I had ever done.

Jack Lalanne agreed with me. The apprehension of coming towards death is sometimes difficult. This is part of my existentialist philosophy.

I will now describe my experiences with women throughout my life. It further illustrates why women are great. I felt this way until a cruel doctor assaulted me and gave me much stinking thinking that caused schizophrenia that I am trying to reverse as much as I can. This stinking thinking and schizophrenia made me a misogynist for a while, someone who does not like women, regardless of sexual preference.

My first good experience with women were my mother and my sisters, who had strengths and loving, a celebration of greatness. I can now return the love. It is a good family to come from. Morality is good for people as long as one's conscience is not trampled on by doctors and educators.

Until I was 13, I did not notice women much. Starting when I was 13, I became interested in women, both physically and socially. I wanted to have more social contact with women, but did not know how to talk to them. My first attempts to approach girls were awkward and I could not hold a good conversation, which is still a problem.

When I was 14, I developed my first crush after having a dream that I was walking hand in hand with a girl, but I did not know how to approach her. I was romantically attracted to girls and fantasized being a hero to them. They liked me somewhat. At this time, a wonderful girl, who showed great compassion that she later used to get into medical school and practice medicine, tried to teach me how to talk. She was very special and she and her friend both made good doctors. My ability to talk was not yet effective, but some girls were sympathetic.

When I turned 15, I became even more romantically attracted to girls and tried to get accepted by them by excelling at football, academics, and physical fitness. I did all my homework and attended all my classes. I was elected president of the class, mostly because the class was female-dominated, and the girls voted for me and the boys voted for the girl who became vice-president as runner-up. This was the best year of my life and women were an important part of it. I also got along very well with my family and was respectful of all of them, after behaviour therapy relieved my severe anxiety and taught me how to talk better.

Half way through the behaviour therapy assertiveness hierarchy, the doctor introduced me to a very intelligent, attractive, interesting, and all-around nice girl who also had difficulty talking. We practiced talking together, supervised by the doctor and she inspired me to complete the hierarchy faster. I liked my sessions with her, and learned much. I had a high regard for her and other women.

The things the doctor said, including his brutal assault, made me into a misogynistic schizophrenic, someone with a painful experience and attitude towards women. It was an anti-exercise, anti-achievement, anti-self-esteem philosophy that caused this. I am trying to reverse his stinking thinking, but it looks like some of the damage is permanent.

When the doctor introduced me to the girl, he said, with an evil grin,

"I think this is going to work out quite well."

He later on gave me her last name, which I used to find her and start dating her, even though he stated that he did not want to play matchmaker. I think he was lying.

The doctor set up a cruel assault, using the separation of my partner's parents to make me feel guilty, and making fun of my guilt, saying it had sexual connotations. He started to criticize my sports, studying, and lack of socialization. He mentioned a lot of schizoid personalities, who did weird things that he would not admit did not apply to me. Eventually he turned to my partner and said,

"This type, of person, is always looking to put himself BETTER than others, like football, kinda snobbish."

Then he said in a low, punishing voice,

"It's not like you at all – studied reflections on other people."

He tried to make me feel as guilty as possible about sports and studying. He might as well have written a prescription for perphenazine at the end of the session, because it has been accurately determined that the assault was exactly what caused my schizophrenia. Also, my other problems of social isolation, schizotypal personality disorder and obsessive-compulsive disorder were severely aggravated, which is what he used as an excuse for the assault. It is like a surgeon cutting off a man's penis, saying he had cancer and the pathology report comes back negative. A doctor should not do something like that even to cure cancer.

Later, when I said that I wanted to get back to what I had in grade 10, he replied that I had not really been doing well then. It is more than the mentally ill that have a distorted perception of reality. I had tremendous potential that was dashed. He said,

"Nope, you're growing up."

In reality, I was growing downward, which is what schizophrenia causes one to do. He was either incompetent or had things in for me. He later probably viewed my time in a concentration camp as getting what I deserved for "acting like Hitler." He liked comparing me to Hitler. I realized later that I did not deserve anything I got in my teens, including the hatred of my relative, guidance counsellor, and especially my principal. The doctor refuses to diagnose or treat my schizophrenia or take responsibility for causing it or the resultant behaviour. One of these behaviours was something the principal of the concentration camp said was a crime and the worst possible crime. I was a destructive little punk who vandalized a school and caused tremendous damage and hijacked an airplane and should have been shot dead immediately. I was scum who did not deserve to live and the principal said,

"You should do something to yourself."

I knew that he was telling me to kill myself. The doctor said that I was lucky to have had the opportunity to be in a concentration camp and just did not make anything of the opportunity. He also said that the idiotic auditory hallucinations of my relative, guidance counsellor, and principal were right because he did not realize that I was hallucinating as a result of schizophrenia. He had said earlier that psychiatry can do great harm even with a highly skilled practitioner. This was an instance just like that. Many people have been ruined by psychiatrists. The one good thing about being in the concentration camp was being exposed to the Quaker religion, which is a wonderful religion, so antithetical to the beliefs of my principal. I, and my wife and fellow Quakers are not the least bit like the lying hypocritical bigot, and his extermination policy.

A doctor who was a Quaker, said,

"This man disgusts me."

He disgusted all the rest of the Quakers who agreed there was no way that he was a Quaker. He was just a sociopath. Anyone who is not disgusted by him is not a decent person.

As mentioned, halfway through grade 11, I started to get abusive with the women at school and home. It was a result of the anti-exercise philosophy as was my later fighting even though I was sometimes in very good condition, these were conative signs of Sz.

After getting over these abusive times, the girls at school knew something was very wrong because I was acting way out of character. In spite of the distress I had caused them, they were sympathetic and made an effort to talk to me. They were very uplifting and I was touched with undying gratitude. I would never again have the same bad attitude towards women or the delusions of grandeur that accompanied it. I made a point of treating them with the dignity and respect that I always had and that they deserve. A bigoted guidance counsellor said out of his hatred for me that this behaviour might come back. He was proven wrong and if he had known me he would have known that his statements were absurd.

My next contact with a woman came at a YMHA dance in the summer of 1975, when I was 22. A very nice and very attractive woman, who turned out to be my age, came up to me and asked,

"Do you want to dance?"

After that, we had several dances together and exchanged phone numbers. I called her and we dated at least once a week, and sometimes more that summer.

She was very kind, gentle, and understanding, in addition to her good looks and we had many good times together. I found it remarkable that she worked full time for 40 years in spite of a handicap that would sideline most people. She re-affirmed my celebration as did the girls in high school. She was and is a true woman of valour, who places a high priority on family. I thought highly of her.

I did not see her much after that summer, and made a point of being aloof until I was 28, in 1982. I abruptly decided that I had better get more involved with women when I became very alarmed in August of 1982 by something that happened while I was taking a course in electron microscopy. I looked around the room and noticed that I was attracted to one of the men. This had never happened before. I checked again by looking at other men in the room and noticed that I was attracted to them as well. After that, I was constantly checking to see if I was still attracted to men and it became a constant obsession as diagnosed by Dr. Kurt Freund, the chief of sexology at the Clarke institute as an obsessive-compulsive disorder. He said that my problem was not homosexuality and I never exhibited homosexual behaviour. It is especially so because it is well known among every serious mental health professional that it is impossible to change one's sexual preference. That I even considered that I was a homosexual is an example of how nasty we sometimes talk to ourselves.

After that I started to date women regularly and pursue women actively and lost my virginity at age 29. The problem finally went away in 1986, around October when I became happy with Diane, who became my girl friend for 18 years, until her cruel death in June, 2001. I replaced my obsession with the tiny bit of attraction we all have for the same sex with an obsessive type of attraction for women that was very strong. I detail this in the chapter, "It Takes A Woman to Help A Man." Female companionship and love relieved me of this very distressing problem.

Diane was a very special woman who brought great joy to her parents and later to me. She was like the ugly duckling who turned into the beautiful swan. Diane was born with Bardet-Biedl syndrome, a rare genetic disorder associated with intellectual problem, deformed hands and feet, motivational problems, large appetite, obesity, and diabetes. Diabetes and kidney failure were the main causes of her death at the tender age of 50. She went into acute respiratory distress syndrome after inhaling some vomit.

Diane's parents were warm, loving kind, and generous both to her and to me, as were her sisters. Diane was in many ways a bright woman who could rise to the occasion. She had excellent conversational skills. She carried the conversation when my cousins came over to dinner. She was like the song, "Honey," She was always young at heart and kinda dumb and kinda smart and I loved her so. Diane showed great personal courage in overcoming her fear of needles and problems associated with dialysis in order to stay alive. She showed "grace under pressure" in many situations. This is in keeping with my existentialist philosophy that it takes courage just to live.

After Diane died in June, 2001, I looked after a cancer patient until he died in November, 2001. From Friday, December 13, 2002 to October 3, 2009, I looked after my mother 24/7 and she did everything to me with Alzheimer's disease that I did to her with Sz, until it became a non issue after I got medicated.

After my mother died, I started to date a wonderful woman who was also incredibly beautiful, and we had a great time together. She had tremendous depth of understanding and said that I was a man, with needs, which she said about my sex drive. She was also a woman, with needs, and was very mature and courageous, a single mother who was very dedicated to her two children. She showed great courage in slapping a man who had threatened her children.

After the extremely beautiful woman, I earned 4,000 dollars doing a research project on the blood levels of Seroquel and used the money to erase debt and join a Chinese dating agency. There, I met a fabulous woman named Kelly. She worked very hard and her determination paid off in her earning enough to become a PSW. She bravely emigrated from China and spread her helping ways wherever she went. She was the kindest, sweetest, most womanly woman I have ever met as well as being very beautiful. She became my fifth sexual partner, and later a fiancee until I had second thoughts. She is one of the fondest memories I have ever had. She also had great intelligence.

My fourth sexual partner was Delia, also from the Chinese dating agency. She was Filipina. She was attractive, but not as much as Denise, Nilani or Kelly. She always criticized me and also my sexual technique so I dropped her.

I then dated a very fine Chinese woman named Sunny. I admire a woman's courage, but I love women who are easily frightened who I can protect. Sunny was afraid of dogs and cars and several other things and said she felt safe with me. I loved that and her. I enjoyed being with her and kissing her. She was very emotionally satisfying. We never went to bed and she was thin, which is not my physical type so I took her picture so I could practice getting an erection for her. I found that when I stopped my morning clonazepam, it worked big time. However, some girls in a drug store told her some lies about me. She took it to heart and told me that she was under too much stress seeing me.

I next did little, but met a wonderful therapist named Alice. We cuddled together a lot and she read many of the books I wrote. She was very beautiful and emotionally satisfying. We had intercourse twice. I got tested for HIV three months later and it came out negative, probably because we always used condoms. She was still a professional and there was a limit to how far I could go with her. She was one of the nicest women I have met, a very caring therapist. She showed great courage in punching a man who would not pay. She took the risk of him coming back and hitting her.

I met my wife, Nilani in March of 2011. I had just earned 5,000 dollars more in the research institute and was sent to Progress Place, a mental health rehabilitation centre after an alcoholic brutalized me. One day, when I was waiting to be let in a beautiful woman boldly walked up to me, put her hand in mine, and asked,

"Want to live together?"

I figured who am I to argue with a lady and said yes. She came up to my condominium and as soon as she stepped through the door, she began taking off her clothes and I found that she was one of the two most beautiful women I had ever seen in my life. We met frequently and got together like that until we were married on October fifth, 2011, after a three day engagement. We have been married ever since. She has schizophrenia, too, and in spite of a few problems, we get along great. Our love grows stronger every day.

She is a great wife, who cooks and makes sure I am dressed and groomed properly. In return, I support her financially and give her a generous spending allowance, gave her a stationary bike, and encouraged her to exercise and join Weight Watchers.

Like me, Nilani came from a dysfunctional family. Unlike me, she had essentially no family. Her parents died in a car accident when she was very young. She was raised by her grandmother, who went into a nursing home when Nilani was ten. She taught Nilani good morals and saw that she did the right thing like going to school. There was an orphan who was raised as her brother and who half-heartedly looked after her for a while. When he got aggressive and yelled at her after much chronic stress, it was the straw that broke the camel's back and caused schizophrenia. She started to hear voices and started laughing and giggling at the voices. Her brother noticed this and astutely knew to take her to the hospital, because she was acting out of character. She was diagnosed and treated for a few months, then bravely emigrated to Canada all by herself. She worked for some cruel people for a while, then led a so-so life in group homes. She said that I am her hero, rescuing her from a bad life. She calls me "Israeli armed commander." She is my heroine, rescuing me from an unhappy life. I am teaching her to be a clinical psychologist, which is difficult because her native language is Tamil. Like me, she got schizophrenia through no fault of her own.

I suggested that my wife take TMS therapy – transcranial magnetic stimulation to get rid of her voices, because it helped me immensely. She said that she needs her voices and delusions in order to function. She enjoys working at Progress Place and we have a great life together. I would like to take her on a vacation, but every day we have together is like a vacation. I think that her history is even worse than mine, but she finds the cruelty of my life hard to believe.

In conclusion, everything that I have known and seen of women confirms that they are the greatest thing ever to grace the planet.

It Takes A Woman To Help A Man - A Triumph Over Sexual Concerns

Ever since I was thirteen, I was strongly attracted to women.. I spent much time fantasizing about them and enjoying looking at them and trying to talk to them. My conversational skills were never good. As mentioned, my sex life consisted almost entirely of fantasy about women until I was 28, when I noticed an attraction towards men for the first time. This turned out to be an obsession with the little bit of attraction that all heterosexuals have toward the same sex. Most people do not notice this attraction because they do not focus on it. The worst thing to do for this problem is to test it or take a great deal of therapy for it. Dr. Aaron M. told me that he had many patients with this problem. He tends to use anti-obsessive medication like clomipramine. All good doctors say that obsessions are very difficult to treat and even with successful resolution there are still some remnants of them.

In retrospect, I now feel that the idea that I was a homosexual was a delusion caused by the schizophrenia and a few psychological factors.

Everyone has a mild attraction towards the non-preferred sex. Homosexuals have a mild attraction towards women. They are often so proud of it that they say that they are bisexual. Human sexual nature is a very unequally weighted bi-sexual nature.

The first doctor that I discusses this problem with was a psychiatrist that I had been seeing for learning problems. He asked,

"What do you think about when you are reading?"

I said hesitantly,

"I think I might be a homosexual."

He launched into a dispassionate way of determining your sexual preference that had to do with one's fantasy life and said that I was probably heterosexual. I found out later that this doctor was a homosexual himself and that he later died of AIDS.

After that, I went to about a dozen doctors and psychologists until I was 32 and my chief complaint was that I was attracted to men. It ended with Dr. Kurt F. chief of sexology at the Clarke institute who told me that he had read every serious study that had ever been done and conducted countless studies himself, and had worked with thousands of homosexuals. He said that the overwhelming conclusion that he and every serious mental health professional had come to was that it was impossible to change one's sexual preference. He said that it was possible for a heterosexual to engage in homosexual behaviour for a while, but that I did not exhibit homosexual behaviour. On questioning, he found that I had had a long history of obsessions, compulsions, phobias, and hypochondriasis. This was no different. To this day, I am still self-punishing and reluctant to be re-assured. I also felt so worthless that no woman would ever want me. After Dr. F. reassured me that I was not a homosexual and could not become one most of what I thought was an attraction to men went away. Dating women, having more to do with them and love and affection also helped a great deal. Finding a girlfriend and a wife was also enormously helpful.

Later on, I realized that the problem with sexual

orientation concerns was caused by schizophrenia. The excess dopamine in the limbic system made me attracted to everything and I was so cruel to myself that I labelled myself a homosexual, which is being inhuman to myself as I have punished myself in many other ways. I am usually my own worst enemy.

My Dear Ones: My Work on Skid Row

"You_Jew, you're going to get your head punched in. You'll be take care of." said the man as he got up to attack me.

In another incident, I had just taken a bottle of liquor from someone, and as I turned to empty it, a bottle of Canadian sherry came flying past my ear. I cleaned up the broken glass and got out as quickly as possible. The man later apologized and explained that he could not control himself when he was drinking. He explained that one of his biggest problems was that he suffered remorse caused by his drunken behaviour. We later became close friends and he always made an effort to tone down his excesses even when he was drunk, although his drinking never stopped. The man from the previous incident also became friendly when physiotherapy gave him hope for a better life. He had previously been friendly, and I will always think of him as his good self.

"Your work with me has given me a whole new lease on life," said another man. Another man who had cursed me up and down about my wanting to give him a bath said,

"Thanks a lot for your help. I feel a lot better now."

These are anecdotes that show that working with alcoholics and skid row people can be very demanding and also very rewarding. The good far outweighed the bad, and the residents of the mission became very dear to me. In the following pages, I will tell of my work with skid row people, set straight some myths and truisms, show some of the humorous and possibly adventurous aspects of working in the home, and hopefully enrich your life as these men enriched mine. These men were graduates of the"college of hard knocks" and taught me a great deal about handling life. They were tough, but kind. They often used foul language, but it usually was not malicious – meaning not directed at or used to hurt people.

The Origin of the Term "Skid Row"

The term, "skid row," came from logging days, about the late 1800s or early 1900s. Loggers would come into town and need a place to stay. Wealthy individuals (in conjunction with religious organizations) would start missions to give lost, uncared for people, sometimes called derelicts, a place to stay. Many of the people staying in missions were loggers and had travelled into town as if they had skid along the logs. They called the travelling along these logs "skid road." This later evolved into skid row just like a prison for people waiting to die is called death row. Skid row did not mean people who had skid to rock bottom, as some people had believed.

It is also important to point out that working with alcoholics and skid row people is not bad, as some people believe. Before I took the job at the mission, a number of people warned me not to take the job because working with skid row alcoholics was just too difficult. I was certainly pleasantly surprised. This was my first full-time well paying job after graduating university and, at first, I took it because I was desperate. But I soon came to enjoy it. Immensely. We had a great bunch of residents, outstanding supervisors to work with and a chance to make a difference in the lives of residents. It gave meaning to my life. This was another reason the residents were very dear to me. In addition, the money that I earned helped me to further my education as it became painfully evident that I needed upgrading for that job.

The Mission and its Purpose

The mission was founded by a religious group in conjunction with the Massey family and several donations in order to provide food and shelter for men who otherwise would not be cared for. It was named after Fred Victor Massey, who was a driving force in creating the mission and died of tuberculosis at age 27. One side of the mission was for transients, mostly younger, but some older who needed a place to provide food and shelter. The side of the mission that I worked on was a home for older men. These men were referred by the hostel for transients, various hospitals and agencies, and any place aware of the mission's services. Ironically, one man was referred to the mission after suffering scurvy. He could have gone to another place, but our mission was chosen because it did not allow drinking. It turned out that the majority of the men were heavy drinkers and the garbage cans were filled to the brim with empty liquor bottles. About two thirds of the residents were active drinkers, and several others had experience with alcohol and either did not drink anymore or drank seldom. Some residents never drank at all. There were very few who did not smoke, and it seemed a miracle that these men lived into their eighties and nineties, one man living to 104. I wondered if this was due to the toughness of the residents or the fact that they did not worry much, or even more likely, natural selection, meaning the strong survive.

Our purpose was not to treat the alcoholism but to provide a good place for the men to stay, to provide good health care and hygiene, and provide food and shelter, and clothing. These factors tended to minimize the harmful effects of drinking. The men who continued drinking did not want to stop.

The administrator was a minister, Reverend Harry Martin, and to this day, I have never worked for a finer man. He was always very kind and generous, eager to listen, and helpful with both personal problems and problems related to work. One of the residents remarked that when they made Mr. Martin they through away the plans. He always made a point of telling people when they did a good job and was very diplomatic when correcting someone's mistake. This was the best way to handle people and he was a master at handling people. A study done showed that people were able to find a specific object much more quickly when they were cheered as they got closer to the object than when they were booed as they got further away from the object. In other words, positive reinforcement works better than negative reinforcement. Mr. Martin always had a great sense of humor and excellent courage in dealing with dangerous situations such as a violent non-resident entering the home. He was also humble enough to do any task such as washing the floor, hanging drapes, or waiting on the men with food.

The head nurse, who supervised me more directly because of her medical knowledge, was every bit as good as Mr. Martin, in her own way. She had a wealth of knowledge that came from forty years in the nursing profession. Four and a half of those years were as a head nurse in intensive care. She was not only good at dealing with people, both patients and staff, but she could spot problems early in their development and prevent them from becoming more serious. For example, one man had deep vein thrombosis, a clot in the large veins of the leg. Dorothy, the head nurse spotted that something was seriously wrong and sent him to the hospital. He was given anti-coagulants that saved his life. Blood clots in deep veins can be thrown into the circulation and damage the brain, heart, and lungs, and kill the person. Dorothy showed great courage in disarming a man with a switch blade when he went to stab another resident in order to gain money for drinking. The man with the switch blade had earlier told me that he would not hesitate to cut someone's throat because he was 84 and could not be put in jail for long. The man was later thrown out and sent to a nursing home where he died.

The home had one orderly on duty in the daytime, one in the evening, and one at night. The head nurse worked Monday to Friday, eight to four. One orderly was a doctor from Hong Kong who was waiting to pass his Canadian licensing exams. The other orderly was someone with a registered nursing assistant diploma from Nova Scotia. There was another orderly who had worked in hospitals for twenty years and picked up a great deal of knowledge. The man who usually did nights was an engineering school dropout. In spite of his lack of medical knowledge, he had common sense and could handle the emergencies that arose. The staff was competent and caring, and helped me a lot.

My own training, at the time was a premedical degree with an emphasis on psychology, science, and health science. I was very enthusiastic and constantly tried to upgrade myself. I certainly needed it. I first took the PSW program, but that was not enough. I audited the paramedic course at a local community college, but it was not until I studied nursing at University of Toronto that I felt I knew enough to look after the residents. The men had many serious medical problems that could cause them a great deal of danger very quickly. As I mentioned, I got a lot of help from the Chinese doctor and head nurse. There was an orderly there who was drunk more often than the residents. He used to confiscate the residents' liquor bottles and drink them himself. I was glad when he was fired.

Most of the men were getting old age pensions or disability pensions, and they received a portion of this each month as "comfort money." The other portion of the residents' income went to running the home. There were subsidies from the government and the United Church. The United Church administrated the home. Every payday (for the residents) many residents would invest their money in alcohol and stay drunk until they ran out of money, usually a week or two after payday. They would be broke and sober for two to three weeks every month. Any time they could get their hands on money, they would go right back to drinking. One of the men would suffer seizures as a result of alcoholic withdrawal, but most of the men functioned well without alcohol. There were no cases of delirium tremens, which is hallucinations caused by alcoholic withdrawal, although some of the men reported previously experiencing that problem. There were many men who suffered brain damage from drinking and became very confused about where they were, who they were, what they were doing, and what was happening in the present. This disorder is an alcoholic disorder called Korsakoff's syndrome because it was described by a Russian named Korsakoff. These unfortunate men did not always have an accurate perception of reality, which is kind of definition of psychosis, and many of the victims knew what was wrong. For example, one of the men said,

"I used to be smart, but my mind is shot from drinking too much." It usually takes many years of heavy drinking for Korsakoff's syndrome to develop.

I do not fully understand why we had so many heavy drinkers in the home, but maybe it was because the men who were drawn to the home had problems that they were trying to solve with alcohol. In doing a study of alcoholism, I found that different people drink for different reasons. We could have ten drinkers in a room and they all would have different reasons for drinking. Drinking should not be looked down on. These men were the backbone of our country. Many of them were veterans. They worked hard and they played hard. I had a great deal of respect for the men in the home. Some people were unfortunate to become alcoholics because they took a drink, liked it and wanted to continue on. There is a theory put forth by an addiction counsellor that talked to alcoholics that they have a different brain chemistry that makes them enjoy drinking. I was fortunate enough that I never liked to drink, but I always said to myself and others,

"There, but for the grace of God go I."

Most of the men, with some exceptions, were likeable drunks.

Incidents and Anecdotes

"You don't have to be crazy to work here but it helps."

This was a sign that I saw on the nursing station of a hospital ward. That would apply to our mission as well. As mentioned earlier, I had a great deal of respect for the men in the home. Nevertheless, they say the darndest things.that can be construed as funny if someone has a sense of humor. The administrator had a good sense of humor and encouraged us to follow him.

One time, there was a fight between two residents. Mr. Martin described to the security guard, saying that Mr. Swanson, a confused man, tried to pick up someone's glasses because he thought they belonged to him. Mr. Iluha intervened and said they were Jimmy's glasses. Everything else normal (Gerry has been drinking). Gerry was Gerry Perk, a leading alcoholic with Korsakoff's syndrome. He could be very funny at times. Every time he drank, he would say,

"Mr. Martin, he was a boxer, said, Gerry, if I catch you drinking, I'm going to punch you right in the nose."

Mr. Martin was a gentle man and would be unlikely to punch anybody.

This man, Gerry Perk, was formerly a talented artist who was paid for his work in drinks because that was all that anyone could afford. In this way, he became an alcoholic. Gerry was always telling people that he worked hard all day painting. In reality, he had been sitting downstairs doing nothing, with a faraway look in his eyes. He frequently came up to Mr. Martin and asked if he could pay for some food. Mr. Martin would set him straight and say,

"Everyone knows Gerry Perk. You've been here for years. Don't worry about food or rent. You're always paid up."

Gerry would say,

"Do you know me?"

Mr Martin would reply,

"Like a book."

Gerry would frequently come and ask what room he was in and we used to anticipate his question and say,

"207, Gerry."

Gerry would walk away, puzzled, wondering how we knew what he was going to ask. Gerry Perk was a likeable man.

Mr. Martin normally detested swearing. One time when Mr. Martin was helping a drunk Gerry Perk to his bed, Gerry said,

"You're a fuck of a good head."

I think that Mr. Martin made an exception about swearing in that circumstance. Gerry P. showed that he appreciated someone caring about him.

Gerry was sometimes afraid of his roommate, who would sometimes get violent when he got drunk. He'd go to Mr. Martin and say,

"That fellow next to me. He's big man. I don't want any trouble."

Mr. Martin would say,

"He's just a little guy. You just have to blow on him and he'll fall apart."

In truth, the man was small and frail and had a

stroke so that he was not very mobile. Gerry would come back and say,

"I don't care how small he is. I don't want any trouble and he seems to want to fight all the time."

We would usually end up sending him up to sick bay until his roommate sobered up.

One of my responsibilities was to look after the residents' personal hygiene such as baths, shaves, and dressing in clean clothes. I went to one man with a change of clothes and told him that I was going to give him a bath. He said,

"I just had a bath."

I said, "When was the last time you had a bath?"

He said, "It was only a month ago."

This man, James W. would often get up in the middle of the night and say,

"I've got to go look after my daughter and grandchildren."

The man next to him would keep up a running commentary and say,

"Can't even look after yourself for Christ's sake."

One night Mr. W. woke up at 3AM and stated that he wanted to go fishing. I don't know what made him say that.

Another time, I caught a man drinking a bottle of alcohol. I told him that we do not allow liquor in the home. He told me to go get the security guard to take away the bottle and that he would not touch a drop until I got back. I went downstairs to get the security guard, and when we came up the bottle was half empty and he was pouring it down for all he was worth. The security guard confiscated what was left of the bottle. A few days later when this man's best friend died, I said,

"I'm terribly sorry, Frank."

He said, "That's okay. I didn't want to drink it anyway."

He did not seem to realize that I was comforting him on the death of his friend.

Meet the Residents: My Dear Ones

One of the greatest joys in life is to help make someone's life a little better. One of the greatest disappointments in life is to fail in this regard. I experienced both in this regard. Here are some case histories to give some idea of what the men in the mission were really like.

The first case history that I will discuss is Mr. Frank I became very attached to him, partly because he was a kind, unselfish man and partly because he needed much care.

One thing that illustrates how unselfish he was occurred after dinner one day. Frank had always had difficulty moving around partly from taking the antipsychotic drug, haloperidol, and partly due to injuries to his knees and hips. I came up and Frank told me that he had used the wastebasket to defecate in because he did not want to make more work for us by messing the bed. This required considerable effort on his part, but as health care workers, we are not looking to have things made easier for us. We are mostly interested in patient welfare.

Even when Frank was dying of stomach cancer, he never complained. When I would ask him how he was, he would say,

"Can't kick."

When he was annoyed, he would say he wouldn't know when asked how he was.

Frank S. was a big, powerful man when he was in his prime. He emigrated from Spain in his early years and was a veteran of World War II. After that, he became a lumberjack and taxicab driver until he retired and moved into our mission. He had some mobility deficits, difficulty moving. Frequently, he had to be cleaned. When he started to have fears of someone stabbing him with a knife, the doctor put him on large doses of haloperidol. He eventually became so immobile that he could not even roll over in bed. He had to be positioned and have his clothing changed often. Even then, he was still wet 95% of the time. After he was taken off the haloperidol, he could walk with the assistance of a cane and did not have significant mobility problems until his cancer progressed to the terminal stages.

Mr. S. was operated on for a benign prostate enlargement and was incontinent for a while after that. At one point, he stopped eating and after several days of this, he asked to go the hospital. I asked the hospital how Mr. Frank was and the nurse replied that he was a very sick man, especially since his bloodwork was all abnormal. Eventually, he was diagnosed with cancer of the stomach, which had spread to several other organs. The surgeon removed some of the cancer from his stomach and closed him up. The doctor also took him off haloperidol, which caused withdrawal symptoms so that Frank felt that he couldn't sleep for several days. After a while, he got used to being on no medication and could sleep, walk about and had no signs of any particular psychiatric problems. Our head nurse decided that none of us should tell him that he was going to die and that way he could enjoy six to eight months of good living.

Mr. Frank did very well for a few months, not drinking but still smoking. He enjoyed life and talked about the days he used to play baseball and do heavy construction work. After about five months, he started to go downhill and could not keep food down. I brought him some Kaiser rolls as he said that he would enjoy them. He continued to vomit and lose weight. He also asked for oxycodone for his "aches and pains" which we were glad to supply, but we knew he was playing down his pain and that it was very bad. He continued to go downhill and asked to be taken to the hospital again. Our doctor told him that there was no point to further surgery as the cancer had spread throughout his body and he would not live more than two or three weeks.

Frank was very angry and said,

"I'm going to have a long rest."

He meant that he was going to die. I tried to see to his needs as best I could, changing his clothes and spending much time with him. At one point, he asked me to squeeze his fingers as they were cold. He probably had a mixture of fear and anger but always managed to smile in spite of the pain, which I am told is like a knife going through you. In the final stages, he had diarrhea and could not move because of the pain so he needed a lot of care. I gave him a wash one night and went to make rounds. When I came back 15 minutes later, Mr. Frank was lying there, stiff, with his eyes rolled back in his head and having no pulse or respiration. I called an ambulance and he was pronounced dead on arrival. He will be sorrowfully missed by those who knew him.

Mr. Fred

Mr. Fred was one of the nicest men I have ever met. He was in most ways a typical resident. He was a true hero from the same mold as the rest of the rest of the residents. He drank heavily and smoked heavily. It caused a stroke in his later years and he had Jacksonian seizures and hemiplegia as a result of the stroke. He once threw a bottle at me for taking away one of his bottles. He followed it up by throwing several more bottles. He was very upset with me for telling the administrator about what he did, because I was frightened, but after a while we became close friends. One could not help liking him. He told me many stories about his past and his coping with the Great Depression. He was very tough mentally and probably physically capable in his younger days. He made attempts to tone down his excesses when he was drunk and very sadly, he suffered remorse about his behaviour while drunk. I thought of a number of ways of dealing with his remorse, but too late. He used to sell seeds for a living. He, unfortunately may not have realized how highly I thought of him. He was one of the finest men I have ever met. He was sent to a nursing home because he could not walk and to rescue him from drinking. When I visited him in Kipling Acres nursing home his drawer was full of alcohol and he hated the nursing home. I lost contact with him for a long time and was very saddened to hear that he had died in his mid-70s.

Mr. John

This was another very fine man and a true hero. He was a veteran of World War 1. He was such a nice man that I could not picture him firing a rifle at someone, but I know how these beliefs can be wrong. He had chronic bronchitis and constantly coughed up green phlegm and had to take antibiotics periodically. His breathing status was a constant concern and it eventually compromised his activities so that food had to be brought up to him. He was a pleasure to look after. He was another man that I had a very high opinion of. His demise came when I left the mission and the people caring for him refused to bring him food. He fell going down to the dining room and died of his injuries.

Mr. Jack Sk.

This man was a Norwegian sailor and a man who worked hard and played hard. He also worked as a steeple jack for a long time. He was a roommate of Mr. John F. and was very pleasant. He was a heavy drinker and I used to wait for him to come in after drinking and give him juice and sandwiches. He had a heart condition and emphysema. He was also a heavy smoker. A few times he went into hypovolemic shock due to overaggressive diuretic therapy to treat his congestive heart failure. He was given much juice in the hospital and this got his blood pressure back up. His condition frightened me a few times and I had to send him to the hospital for a heart attack one time. He died after I left the home.

Mr. Jim

This man was a kind of Jekyll-Hyde personality. He had a good side and a bad side that were complete opposites. Most of his bad side would come out when he was drinking. This man would sculpt pots for flowers and look after the plants. He sold the plants to raise more money for drinking. He was as powerful as a pocket Hulk and used to help people with heavy lifting. He once helped to lift Mr. Sanchez up some stairs, wheelchair and all. He said,

"We should take him over to Canada Packers and sell him."

He was Irish, and some people would say that being Irish accounted for his bad temper. I have known many Irish people who do not have bad tempers.

One day, Mr. Jim M. came in from an evening of heavy drinking at the bar down the street and started cursing the security guard because it took him a few seconds to answer the door. The security guard called Mr. Martin and said,

"I don't have to take that."

Mr. Martin then called me and asked,

"Peter, can you tell me what's going on?"

I started saying that I was giving Mr. Watson a bath and...

Fortunately, a residing supervisor came on the phone and explained what happened because I did not know what happened until she explained.

Another time, Mr. Jim M. came back from a night of heavy drinking and the security guard watching was gone. This infuriated the man so he grabbed the nearest and started shaking him viciously. He also started banging tables and chairs and swearing. He then went upstairs to sleep off his drunkenness.

When we went up to see the resident who had been shaken, he was so frightened that he was shaking like a leaf. We were very concerned because the man had a heart condition. Earlier, he had taken a frail, elderly man and dashed him into the ground. He also beat up one of the orderlies. Several times, I had stepped in front of him to prevent him from attacking various residents and if I had been on hand for this latest incident, it might not have happened. I wrote a detailed report, which Mr. Martin read the next day and gave Mr. Martin a verbal report that night. He promised drastic action.

The plan was to send Mr. M. to a treatment centre for alcoholics that had very pleasant surroundings. Mr. Martin felt that he would like it. When Mr. M. would not go there because he did not want to stop drinking, he was discharged from the home. I saw him selling flowers a few months later and asked how he was doing.

He replied, "I'm growing old gracefully."

He could have been a good resident if we could accentuate his positive characteristics and eliminated the negative. This would not be the last time I would have let someone by not being there when I was needed.

Mr. Don

This man presents a very happy story. He lived to be 104 years old and was strong and active until he was 100. He always went around saying,

"I feel like I did when I was 50."

He did not smoke or drink and watched his diet as carefully as he could. Before he came into the home, he was a vegetarian and only ate meat twice a week. When he came into the home, he had to eat meat at almost every meal because that was what was being served, but he would skip a meal if it was too salty. He had the legs of a football player and prominent biceps as well as rippling muscles. He had only a slight amount of fat on his belly. Until he was 99, he walked five miles every day. He had worked at coal shovelling until he retired at age eighty-four.

Mr. Don did not stop with his physical fitness regimen until age 99, when he slipped on some ice and broke his hip. He was sent to a hospital and not given physiotherapy. This caused the tendons in his leg to shorten so that they were stuck in a bent position called a contracture. Because of that, he could not walk anymore and went downhill.

Mr. Don had some interesting ideas on how to take care of himself. In addition to diet and exercise, he believed in the use of lanolin for infections (which is not a good idea). He used Vicks products for many ailments with good results and credits them with saving his life when he had a bout of pneumonia. He was a walking advertisement for Vicks products.

One time I had to put antibiotics on his toes because he thought he was caring for his toes by pulling his toenails off. Unfortunately, he got an infection. Fortunately, it was resolved.

Mr. Mitchell loved most sports and listened to football, soccer, and hockey games. He himself had played many sports, including lacrosse when he was younger. He could keep a visitor talking for hours. His medical was usually summed as "very fit for age." Even though he led a long, happy, and healthy life, he will still be missed.

Mr. John S.

John S. was another resident who did not smoke or drink. He was a very likeable man who endeared himself to many people. In his younger days, he did manual labour, working 14 to16 hours on a farm near Ottawa.. He was in good condition when he was working, but his epilepsy, decreasing mobility, and lack of balance caught up with him.

Earl stated that wherever there was a floor, you did not trust John S., meaning that he would fall whenever he would take his eyes off the floor, which happened often. We never really found out what happened to his balance, but it was probably caused by damage to the balance centre in his brain.

Mr. S. had an operation on his elbow to correct numbness in his fingers. The operation helped because it restored nerve transmission from his elbows to his fingers, but the operation left his arm stiff and sore. I did range of motion exercises with him in order to get rid of the stiffness and consequently the pain. After a while he got better.

In his last two years, Mr. S. became incontinent of urine and feces for some reason, and frequently had to be cleaned up. Because there were so many residents needing care, we could not wash and change him often enough to prevent skin rashes. Mr. S. was always pleasant through all his ordeals and I was sorry to hear of his demise a few years later

Big Earl

He stood six foot four weighing 225, kinda broad at the shoulder, kinda narrow at the hip, and everyone knew you didn't give no lip to Big Earl. After several years of enjoying food, Earl finally put weight on his middle, but once was a tapered, powerful athlete. In his younger days, he worked at many strenuous manual labour jobs such as coal mining, construction, and ditch digging. He was a veteran of the professional wrestling ring and played football for the Hamilton Tiger Cats in Canada. He had to work in a steel mine as well because football and wrestling did not pay well at that time. He was also a military policeman in World War II. He had a loud, booming voice at times and commanded a great deal of respect. One day, about two weeks after he went to visit his daughter in Columbus, Ohio, I was eagerly awaiting his return. When I was delivering some tea on the third floor, I could hear his voice from the bottom of the building and I knew that Big Earl was back.

Earl had led a full life in many ways. He had a university education as an engineer and worked at that for a long time. He had several girlfriends and a few wives, the odd one being common law. He had had a drinking problem at one time, but he overcame it and was very proud of his sobriety. He even came to look down on drinking and said some negative things about alcoholics at times. Earl also overcame a serious stroke at age 49. After several years he went back to work. He did not stop working until he had a heart that required insertion of a pacemaker. He was a heavy smoker and had serious chronic obstructive lung disease, which he eventually died of. With this disease, the air sacs in the lungs break down and there is less area for gas exchange with the blood. This disease puts a strain on the heart because it is difficult for the heart to push blood through damaged lungs. This strain can make the heart unable to do its job so that blood backs up first in the jugular vein, the liver, then the tissues. It is called heart failure.

Getting back to Big Earl and his courage, he had several painful medical problems while at the mission such as a bowel obstruction, but did not utter so much as a whimper. Earl was elected president of the resident's council, probably because he was one of the few educated men there. Some people were asked who the administrator of the senior citizen's home was and said,

"I thought it was Mr. Earl," jokingly.

I often visited Earl when I needed a lift and he would always supply pleasant conversation. I always had to make sure he was well supplied with Beclovent and Ventolin inhalers, and I tended to keep an eye on him, generally. He needed a lot of care, partly because he needed ointment on his foot ulcers and partly because of his fragile medical condition. An interesting thing about him is that he sometimes got his words mixed up. He sometimes called Mr. Westergaard, Mr. Overgaard, and valisone G was valenG. This was probably from his old stroke.

Earl lived to be 76, surviving several scrapes. At one point, his lungs were so bad that only two areas the size of a woman's fists were working. That was successfully treated, but I always worried about him. He was one of the finest men I have ever met.

Mr. Jim P.

This was an interesting man. He was very tough and unselfish. He once said,

"I hope things get better for the younger people of this country. Things were not very good for me, but I had my shot at life."

Mr. P. suffered from rheumatoid arthritis that became very painful in his last few years. He said that sometimes all he could do for the pain is get drunk. He had nodes and deformities on most of his joints. He used to like to watch wrestling at Maple Leaf Gardens and have a few beers while he was out. He would come back for large doses of antacids to get rid of the sore stomach caused by the beers.

Here was a man who had been a lumberjack all his life and worked despite great pain. He was one of the persons who skid row was named after as mentioned earlier. He was usually good-natured and joking, but he became very cantankerous when his arthritis got bad. He ended up having a heart attack and getting over it. His arthritis ruined his appetite so that he lost about 100 pounds.

He became very sour on everyone, due mostly to his arthritis and one day left for Sudbury to get away from all the "bad people." He ended up dying of a fatal heart attack there and if I knew him, he sent away anyone trying to help him. He was a good friend most of the time and told me that I took good care of him. He cared about the other residents and urged the man on duty to do something about his roommate, Mr. Joe S., who was unusually restless. The man on duty was on loan from an agency and did nothing. Mr. Joe died probably due to congestive heart failure causing pulmonary oedema. I let Mr. him down because if I had been there that night, he might not have died.

Joe

Joe was also interesting. He was a very heavy drinker and justified his drinking as a cure for his dizziness. He had Meniere's disease, which is an ear infection that damages balance and hearing, functions partially controlled by the ear. Joe's disease did not bother him too much unless he was drinking. He said that his ear was blocked making his brain turn around. He was willing to try anything to cure it, especially drinking. Joe was deaf and particularly had difficulty hearing when you told him what he did not want to hear like, "It's time for your bath." I could usually get through to him by writing notes or talking loudly.

Joe eventually developed hepatitis from drinking. His eyeball turned yellow and he developed such a severe stomach bleed that his hemoglobin dropped to one third of the normal level. The hemoglobin, which carried oxygen in the blood, being low cause the blood vessels to the heart to dilate, causing heart failure by overloading the heart.

Joe was a good friend and never caused any trouble, drunk or sober. He had smelly sores on his skin from psoriasis, but as long as we put cortisone on them regularly, they were not too bad. We left a bottle of cortisone by his bed, but he cared about himself so little that he never used it.

Myths and Truths About Alcoholism

One statement made about drinking problems is that in order to quit, one must stop drinking entirely. I found that with most of the men in the home, they fell into a number of groups. One group would drink at every opportunity. These men were not motivated to quit. However, few of them would show signs of missing alcohol if they could not get it. They just carried on their normal lives. Another group would stop for the most part and only occasionally drink. Few of the men were social drinkers. Once they took a drink, they would usually lose control and get drunk.

Another statement is that once someone achieves sobriety, he loses his craving for alcohol. This looked to be true for the most part, especially when people are proud of their sobriety, like Earl Nevills.

Reformed alcoholics often resent being called alcoholics.

Also true is that alcoholics cannot stop after their first drink.

Another true statement is that alcoholics do not necessarily have more problems than most people.

I also found that alcoholics' families were sometimes negative towards them, especially when they caused them nothing but trouble.

Some people think that alcoholics are embarrassing and difficult. In some of the men, alcohol brought out the worst in them. Most of our guys were likeable drunks.

A myth about alcoholism is that their drinking is secretive. This was not true of the men in the home.

One thing that I found about the men in the home is that they encouraged other people to drink. They would encourage each other to drink and offered me drinks sometimes, which I always refused.

There are just as many alcoholics among wealthy and middle class people as poor people.

The most important point is that alcoholics are usually likeable people.

Lasting and My Stoical Fortitude

<u>The 3-12 Program</u>

Exercise 1 – Heart Power – lift knees and swing arms to march in place. Continue for 10 minutes.

Exercise 2 – crunches – lie on back, feet flat on floor, hands clasped behind head. Curl up trunk and down again for one repetition

reverse crunches – same as above, only draw knees up towards chest and down again for one repetition.

Exercise 3 – pushups – prone position, hands under shoulders, push up to arms extended and down again for one repetition.

<u>Isometrics</u>

- neck pushes with hands, against front, back, and sides.

- Arms in front and squeeze

- push against side of knees

- back to wall, press hands against wall with triceps.

- Press down on knees

- Shoulder shrug on chair.

- Curl biceps through range of motion

- sit ups

- squeeze rubber balls.

- Press down on chair.

- Hand over head squeeze
- rope pull apart and resist, hands at belly
- belly press inward with hands
- pull towel apart, hands overhead
- pull towel apart, arms straight, at chest level.
- Pull towel apart, belly level
- pull towel apart, hands behind you.
- Resist hand near head, both hands, pull felt in bicep
- hands press on side of door.
- Squeeze books
- try to bend steel bar

Weights

- overhead press
- biceps curl
- triceps push back
- upright row
- shoulder shrugs
- elbows above head, hands at shoulders, and press.
- Bent arm row with dumbbell, one hand on chair
- push ups

- crunches and reverse crunches

Ridding Fear and Pain

- Find irrational, catastrophic thoughts and say, Stop!
- Relax muscles
- Admit information from senses – sight, hearing, touch, muscle position awareness, smell, taste
- Dwell in the here and now.

In chair or bed, slow down your breathing from 16-20 breaths per minute to 3-6 times per minute. Then muscle relaxation. Wrinkle forehead for 5 secs., relax 30 secs. Tense and relax neck in same way. Then chest, abdomen, back, arms, legs,feet, and hands

Think of sights and sounds of beauty.

Let the bad thoughts float out of your body and good thoughts flow in.

Visualize good things happening.

Self-hypnosis – Stare at your thumbs, relax completely and count from 3 to 1. At 1, you will be asleep. Now you are in a focused trance. Give yourself the suggestion that every time you take a slow, deep breath, you will relax and achieve whatever you want. Count from 0 to3 and come out of the trance feeling good.

There are also certain suggestions that are helpful such as muscle heaviness, muscle softness, and a sensation of letting go. A sensation of warmth and tingling in your skin and muscles is helpful. Also, becoming aware of your body and internal organs and body functions is for anxiety reduction.

Some Suggestions for Relaxation and Exercise

For exercise, do 12 minutes of walking, swimming, or running. Follow that with 16 minutes of interval training. Do 30 to 60 seconds of intense exercise followed by 2 minutes of recovery at a lighter pace for two minutes. Then finish with 12 minutes of moderate exercise as at the beginning for a total of 40 minutes.

For relaxation, work from the outside in. Sit back comfortably in the chair, let your skin get looser, looser, looser. Let your muscles go completely limp. Let your joints get further and further apart. Let your bones get softer, softer, softer. Let your heart go soft and your blood vessels dilate. Generate a tingling in your hands and feet. Slow down a nerve message from your head to your toes from 120 ft./sec to 119.9 ft./sec. Let your internal organs relax. Let your arms and legs get heavier and warmer. Now be supremely calm.

I have found these suggestions helpful. I hope you do, too.

How to Help Yourself Have A Good Life In Spite of Mental Illness

- Stay physically fit. Develop your strength, endurance, and flexibility as much as possible.

- Notice when you feel distress and seek help. If the helper disrespects you, dump him and seek someone else.

- Look to when you were happy and successful and see if you are different. Try to mimic success.

- Be gainfully employed as much as possible.

- Try to develop your education as much as possible.

- Have a financial plan. Try to spend as little as possible.

- Do not waste time on hopeless problems. Accept them and do something else. For example, my learning/cognitive deficit.

- Stay hopeful and optimistic. Do not listen to naysayers, bullies,and negative people. An optimistic attitude is the healthy one.

- If an idea gives you distress, it is almost certainly unhealthy, unrealistic, and non-constructive.

- Do not live for others. Please yourself and follow your dreams and principles.

- Keep getting up after being knocked down.

- Never quit.

- Develop a passion and pursue it. These may change from time to time. Make your goals realistic

- Be a friend to others, especially people you like.

- Socialize, but do not force yourself.

Only do it if you like it. Practice assertiveness.

- Avoid mean and negative people and tell them off if necessary.

- Do not blame yourself for problems not under your control.

- Take medication as prescribed for your health and good behaviour.

- Research your problems and find solutions.

- Develop your life from several angles and areas.

- Believe in a higher power and spiritual side.

- Be objective, detached, and comforting about all sensory hallucinations. Do not accept them. Dispute voices you hear, but do not dwell on them.

- Ask yourself if distressing beliefs are realistic or part of your disease.

- Do not listen to doctors who run down fitness. They and anyone with this belief are wrong, dangerously so.

- Do not let anyone let you do, think, believe or feel something that you do not want.

- Do not listen to criticism, punishment, or brutalization. These are evil people who deserve what they say you deserve.

- Relax, keep calm, feel good, do therapy,

and do not ruminate or use social comparison.

How to Help Others With a Mental Disease

- Be gentle. Do not assault them or make them do things they do not want as I was.

- Do not laugh, gossip, or make fun of them.

- Be empathetic. Try to put yourself in their shoes.

- Do not run them down. Build them up.

- Take genuine interest in them.

- Look for ways to help them.

- Recognize if they are in distress or non-responding to treatment.

- Recognize if they are acting out of character.

- Do not diagnose them if you are not qualified.

- Do not look down on them

- Be in favour of exercise.

- Do not deny their knowledge, ability, or potential. Respect them.

- Welcome their help seeking

- Do not reject them.

- Be friendly.

- Be open-minded. They are not strange, bizarre, or heinous, or dangerous.

Living Better Magnetically

Transcranial magnetic stimulation is a great breakthrough in modern psychiatry. One of the pioneers is Dr. Jeff Daskalakis, a courageous, caring and compassionate doctor, who also happens to be an excellent clinician.

I was first introduced to TMS therapy as an experiment on ridding auditory hallucinations. It is given by magnetic coils on the temporal lobe, the auditory centre of the brain. I took 1 hr. of treatment, 5 days a week for four weeks. After a few days, the nasty voices started to break up. By 1 month, they were almost gone. 2-3 months after the therapy stopped, the voices were gone and only occasionally came back. I was delighted. It made a huge difference in my life and everyone said I was much calmer. TMS therapy on the temporal lobe has a side effect of a feeling of well-being.

TMS therapy on the frontal lobes is helpful for depression as long as the person does not have schizophrenia.

Later, I mentioned to Dr. Daskalakis that the voices sometimes came back as obsessive thoughts. They went away by the time I saw him.

A little later, I was diagnosed with major depressive disorder, that aggravates the negative symptoms of Sz. I took magnetic seizure therapy for the problem. It uses magnetic stimulation of the frontal lobe to induce a seizure. It is good for major depressive disorder, obsessive-compulsive disorder, schizophrenia, and post-traumatic stress disorder. I had all four and it helped immensely. I had ten treatments and the only thing I did not like was being anesthetized.

Today, I am so free of symptoms that I say that life begins at 60. Bless you TMS researchers.

The Joy of Skydiving

Skydiving can be an awesome experience. I was able to partake of this thanks to Adam Mabee, Andrew Lee, Elena, and the wonderful staff at the parachute school of Toronto. This facility is located northeast of Newmarket, near Sutton, Ontario, in the small country of Baldwin, Ontario. I first got interested in skydiving after hearing about it from a friend. It sounded like a normal thing to do after a lot of abnormal things I had done, previously. It became stronger and stronger in my mind until it reached a peak one day. Previously, I had taken training for a solo jump in February, 2012, but the instructor, concerned for my safety, and possibly saving my life, would not let me jump because I could not learn the proper technique due to the learning disability/cognitive deficit discussed earlier. At the time, I was a little deflated going home.

My fabulous wife, who is extremely beautiful, brainy, and brave did not want me to jump out of an airplane. She said she needed me and what would happen to her if I died. However, I had a low opinion of myself that needed bolstering by action. Skydiving proved to be the perfect therapy. It has made me appreciate her wonderful qualities much more because I have a higher opinion of myself. Also, I am more relaxed and content. Like I said when I first met my wife,

"I feel like I have never been hurt in my life."

The experience of skydiving made that much stronger.

When you go skydiving, you are essentially jumping to your death. If you are lucky, this is prevented by your parachute. There is no guarantee that the parachute will open, due to the possibility of human error that can occur at any stage of the jumping process, including packing, flying the plane, and the jumping process. Skydivers take their lives in their hands day in and day out. I salute them. Skydiving instructors, such as the extremely brave Andrew benefit many people.

A few days before the jump, I started practicing relaxation techniques regularly. Because I was rusty at it, I had difficulty getting my level of anxiety down. After the jump, my wife said that she could tell that I had been anxious the previous few days, even though I tried to hide it.

On the day of the jump, I woke up early and carried a 21 pound pack for an hour. I did all the relaxation techniques that I could think of, but was disappointed that anxiety still crept through. The relaxation techniques work better if you do them regularly when you are not anxious. I paid my bus fare, hopped in the bus and a few minutes later, we were off. I felt almost certain that I would not be coming back. I was very worried about my wife, and had transferred all the money from my account to hers, but I was determined to make the jump.

All through the trip, I looked at the beautiful scenery and did my relaxation. This time it was working and I felt relatively good. I arrived in Sutton and phoned Adam. He said,

"Holy smokes, you're early!" "I'll be there to pick you up in 20 minutes."

Half an hour later, a very nice man came to greet me and said,

"Peter, I'm Adam."

We shook hands and I said that I was pleased to meet him. The scenery continued to be beautiful with green leaves, tall trees, a blue sky, some wispy clouds, a warm, yellow sun, and a very invigorating smell to the air, with Lake Simcoe being nearby. It was all like a tonic. Also, I should mention that the Parachute School of Toronto has seldom had injuries or deaths. They have the best safety record going.

Adam took me to the school, which was a quaint, old place with a cottage, hay, airplanes, and picnic tables. He introduced to a very beautiful and kind woman named Elena. She turned out to be very brave as well as she was a good skydiver. I had a strong feeling when I met her that would be the case. She helped me with some paperwork and watching a movie explaining the dangers of skydiving. Aside from my fear of dying, chickening out was probably my greatest fear. I had a mortal fear of chicken.

When Elena introduced me to a very kind, cheerful, and friendly man named Andrew, who had an English accent, my fears were relieved. I knew there could be no fear of chicken with such a fearless man nearby.

There was also a very beautiful woman, named Margo, I think, who wanted to get back to skydiving after recovering from some injuries. Beauty seems to run among skydivers. I remembered Dr. Joseph Wolpe's ideas on reciprocal inhibition therapy for anxiety. A beautiful woman could make you feel better. It worked.

As we went up in the airplane, I began to feel better knowing I would make the jump, but felt an unpleasant feeling of the ground being so far away. I felt like I would have preferred to jump at 3000 feet.

That looked alright. We climbed to 14,000 feet. I felt alright and pushed toward the opening of the plane and out. I arched my back and spread my hands and legs and tried to pretend that I was Superman. However, Superman had no need for fear.

After about a minute of freefall, the parachute opened and I knew I was mostly home-free. I had an unpleasant feeling of rising at first and tried a few turns and manoeuvres. Some of them felt a little rough.

When I saw the ground approaching, I felt elated. When I touched down and did my landing procedure, I felt elated and grateful to have made it down in one piece. I felt better and better and may feel better for a long time, if not for the rest of my life. Bless you, Adam, Andrew, Elena, and the Parachute School of Toronto.

The Physical and Spiritual Qualities of Nilani Universe-Cohen (Chesty)

Nilani looked incredibly beautiful standing there in her purple dress. It was hard to believe that she had not descended from the heavens. Her long, brown hair fell like eye candy beyond her shoulders to the middle of her back and her face was radiant and gorgeous, especially when she smiled. Her complexion was dark, like chocolate ice-cream and her skin looked good enough to eat. Her face was the most beautiful part of her and reflected her soul, but there is more. Her feet were pretty, her legs were juicy, well-sculpted and sexy, and her belly was luscious. Her arms were full and impressive, showing a feminine strength in them. If one touched her, he would know that he touched a woman. Her arms were capable of a tremendously powerful and affectionate hug, one of her many virtues. Her magnificent breasts swelled out from her chest like mountains against the rolling landscape of her body. They resembled watermelons that had been peeled succulently. She looked more like a love goddess, or Venus. It was easy to see why she was the reigning and lifetime Miss Universe, someone I am very lucky to know.

However great her physical qualities are, they are dwarfed by her spiritual and mental qualities. She has tremendous intelligence and depth of perception and understanding. She understands me as few have ever done. She has compassion for minorities, the unfortunate, and for me. She is hard-working as a homemaker, employee, and student and does not have a lazy bone in her body.

She is one of the most beautiful women and greatest lovers of all time, a powerful teacher of techniques and ideas. She is tremendously feminine and can make a man feel like a man. Life has not been kind to her and she has had tremendous problems to overcome. She has had incredible courage in overcoming these problems. She is totally unspoiled and has no bitterness about her past or resentment for anyone. She is the greatest woman and wife of all time.

Why All People are Great

Human beings are the noblest of God's creatures because they have choice, reason, social interaction, and can do constructive works. All God's creatures are creatures of good, but mankind, especially females are great. People who destroyed the health, lives, and well-being of us are simply good people gone astray. They could have been as great as the vast majority of mankind. Man was created in the image of God and the light of God shines in all human beings and as such we are all great. This applies to beggars, people dependent on social service, as well as working, self-supporting, and wealthy people.

Men of opposite sex orientation still help other men socially. Men of same sex orientation help all men socially and some men in a special way. This can similarly be said of women of same and opposite sex orientation.

All people have their strengths and weaknesses, without fail and by focusing on the strengths of people and their good sides, rather than their weaknesses we can make them great. For example, one of my strengths is an exceptional drive to accomplish set outcomes. This has a downside of a bad temper, which sometimes shows. However my good side is far more important than my bad side.

It is said that courage makes a hero and that the difference between a hero and an altruist, someone interested in helping others is one of degree. Since it takes courage just to live, therefore we are all heroes and all of us are great.

Some people are leaders and some people are followers and neither can exist without the other. This is another reason why all of us are great.

Some people leave works such as scientific discoveries and literature that go down to posterity. However, as in saving lives, this is like winning a lottery. The chances of it happening are the same as being struck by lightning twice. The vast majority of people are great by their interaction with other people. Also, what one considers a great achievement, another would play down and vice versa. Some of my writing has helped some people as has some of the work I have done, but just not on the grand scale as people like Louis Pasteur, Ernest Hemingway, Isaac Asimov, and others who went down to posterity. The difference between a little guy like me and these other people, again is one of degree. Everything we think, say or do, with emphasis on the latter two, is etched permanently on the infinite space-time continuum and noted by God.

Also, we are all interconnected and have more similarities than the inevitable differences, so our similarities to these conventionally great people make us great.

We are all bound in our common humanity, our universal similarities, and our differences, which we all have. Dr. Eben Alexander, a neurosurgeon and skydiver, wrote about his becoming brain dead and going to heaven, said that we all come from heaven before we are born and we all go to heaven after we die. We are all bound in our common mortality, which is not hard to prove. I compare myself to some people and other people can compare to others.

I have a friend with bipolar affective disorder, who showed great courage in battling back from a devastating stroke, and bipolar affective disorder whose accomplishments can be compared to Helen Keller. She also had great beauty, which some women do not acknowledge in themselves. This is more evidence of our common greatness.

All my patients have been very dear to me and have helped me like I have helped them. Greatness is our common bond of humanity. Some people are helpers who need the people they help as much as the people they help need them. This is shown in the chapter My Dear Ones. My patients were all heroes who made me feel like a hero for knowing them.

Getting back to the start of this article, the belief that the light of God shines in all people eternally leads to mutual respect for each other so that we will only do good things for each other and not harm each other. We must also recognize that the light of God shines in ourselves and look after ourselves. Some doctors, educators, and family members have not subscribed to the belief that the light of God shines in all people and have done great harm. To help one person is to help millions and to harm one person is to harm millions. No man is an island, entire unto himself, and we are all immensely important as parts of the human race.

Man is interconnected and interdependent in

many ways. Man is definitely a social animal. Even people who seem to be independent such as hermits who live alone in the wilderness are social and connected because their behaviour is based on previous interactions with other people. Feral children, who have grown up with no contact with humans do not live very long. Similarly, solo sex is based on fantasies of other people, even though it seems like a solo activity.

My fabulous wife who looks after me with saintly dedication, and copes with a tough disease, is the most beautiful woman I have ever seen and helps me as importantly as some people have helped millions. Fantasies often turn into reality.

A bird who was lying with his feet in the air was asked what he was doing.

He said, "I am holding up the sky because I heard it was falling."

The person said, "You cannot hold up the sky."

The bird replied, "One does what one can."

People who have achieved great things have done what they can and others of seemingly modest achievement are great because they do what they can. People of seemingly low achievement, such as myself are simply less fortunate than people with better health or abilities. My life story and accomplishments are written here.

A man travelled a long distance to see a holy man. He came to the house and encountered a servant who said, "Thank you for coming. Good-bye."

He said, "But I came to see the holy man."

The servant replied, "You already have."

Every person you meet, whether in rags or well-dressed, rich or poor, young or old, learned or uneducated, male or female, sick or healthy, attractive or plain, well-mannered or ill-bred, boisterous or soft-spoken is a holy person. Everyone is wholly human. Everyone is a teacher. Our greatness is inherent in our humanity.

Work History

1978 -1981 – Evening supervisor, Fred Victor Mission

1981 – 1984 – Health care aide, Comcare and St. John's Rehabilitation hospital

1984- 1986 – Porter, Grace hospital, Toronto

1986- 1991 – Editor, Hogrefe and Hans Huber publishers, Toronto

1991- 1999 – Telephone interviewer, Infogroup, Toronto

1999- 2001 – Private practice, anxiety and suicide counselling, life coach, Toronto

2001 – 2002 – Health care aide for man with cancer

2002- 2009 – caregiver 24/7 for mother with Alzheimer's disease

2010- 2012 – Tutor for Brilliant Tutors

1984-   - Writer

2014- 2016 – Customer Service Ambassador, TTC

Education

Certified in CPR and first aid many times, saved

a life with CPR

personal fitness training diplomatic audited

paramedic course. Humber College

Advanced Cardiac Life Support, University of Toronto

B.A. - science and psychology

2 years nursing, University of Toronto before had to leave due to cognitive deficit

PhD in health science and psychology

Leadership Role

- Showed superior judgement and quick thinking in medical emergencies which saved lives.

- Responsible for the Fred Victor Mission for the physical and emotional well-being of 67 resident's 2/3 being critically ill and most being alcoholics.

- Demonstrated resoluteness in managing stressful and aggressive behaviour of residents to maintain their overall health.

- Displayed compassion and kindness with aggressive behaviour.

- Liaised with other health care providers as necessary.

Publications

- Boldly Travel Hero – pending
- Published – The Brain In Pain – Iguana books, 2012
- Self-published – It Takes A Woman, 2011
- Published – Kidneys, Craziness, and Courage – X-Libris, 2011
- Self-published – Hope and help for mental illness
- Self-published Dr. Peter Cohen's Program for Increasing Successful
- Published Striving for Peace and Tolerance, Amazon, 2010
- Self-published – How to Improve your Mental and Physical Fitness
- Self published – Fitness
- Published- From Mad to Glad – Volumes Publishing, Kitchener
- Self-published – You Don't Have to Suffer

The Barbarism of Conscience

It is well known by anyone who knows psychology, psychiatry, or psychoanalysis that the conscience is a barbaric structure. It, when used the wrong way was a major factor in causing my schizophrenia. Another way, I experienced is that it caused my masochism, which I have experienced since I was very young. It often takes the form of a sexual perversion, and also a sick desire for bad luck and a feeling that I do not deserve to live. Masochism is just one of the illnesses that conscience can bring on. Depression is another one. Although depression resulting from guilt only occurs in adults and rarely in adolescents as it is a sign of maturity, it is undesirable. The reason that guilt-related depression only occurs in adults is because our conscience constantly gets stronger as we get older. Our conscience gets stronger until the day we die. Also, impulse control gets stronger until the day we die. However, there are great limits to what conscience and impulse control can accomplish. Conscience normally gives us control over ourselves. However, too much control over ourselves causes feelings to build up until they explode. Also, depression as any mental illness causes us to act less maturely.

Another bad effect of conscience occurs when our primitive passions manipulate it. An example would be a religious figure who punishes people whom he believes to be evil, but really is only acting out of hatred. I once had a principal who was like this. He used my conscience to punish me and try to induce me to suicide and cause tremendous distress. It did permanent damage and caused post-traumatic stress disorder. These acts of barbarism will forever stand as his shame, as Tony Blair said of Osama Bin Laden. My principal believed in guns and murder to combat the scourge of fighting. In order to have his way, everyone would carry a gun and use it if someone tried to assault him. He would then kill the person and be hailed a hero. Since 50% of schizophrenics have struck out at someone at some point in their life, he would like to round up all schizophrenics and machine gun us all down. He used to encourage other students to bully me and punch me because of his hatred of violence. He hated violence like Adolf Hitler hated the Jews. He was an enormous hypocrite and the most violent person I have ever seen. The police hated him. Disciplinarian murderers of prostitutes are like this. Fortunately, he never became leader of a country like Adolf Hitler, but he was well-respected among educators.

Conscience is also bad because we use guilt to remove guilt. A cruel doctor made me feel guilty about sports and studying in a brutal assault that he set up. This assault led me to committing a string of crimes and caused me to be saddled with schizophrenia for the rest of my life. However, we must play the hand we're dealt. Everyone has some cross to bear.

People who are less mature and have weak consciences tend to learn from their mistakes and be more objective. They eventually settle down and become good people once they mature. People with strong consciences are too mature already and need therapy in order to feel better, although sometimes it does not help.

Some people are so misguided that they feel guilty about things that are not their fault. For one thing, they may feel guilty about things that are not under their control. Also, they may feel guilty about acts caused by a mental illness that they are not responsible for.

Some people's consciences are so warped that they feel guilty about just having the thought of doing something wrong. Psychopaths can slash off someone's head and not feel anything. The other extreme is feeling guilty about just saying something to somebody.

Guilt causes resentment about its origin and causes us to hold grudges. It leads to a dislike of people and lack of reverence for life. Guilt is a scourge like any disease.

A reasonable amount of guilt is good provided that it does not cause one to suffer and provided it can be used in a constructive way. Other people with weak consciences are more likely to do things wrong than guilty people.

Guilt is not useful to prevent transgressions. It only makes us irritable so that we are more likely to transgress. Letting go of guilt and using love to prevent transgressions works much better. This has been my experience. Guilt interferes with love and all that is good.

The primitive drives that we all have are constantly at war with the conscience to see who wins. Together they threaten to drown out reasoning and make us lose touch with reality in a dangerous way. We must use reason to override guilt and primitive passions. Reason points the way to good behaviour.

Guilt is anger directed toward oneself and can be easily directed toward others. Also, when you have a bad thought that you want to get rid of, guilt is the energy for the repetition of that thought because it energizes the same neural circuitry. For example if you have a pedophiliac thought that you want to get rid of, guilt is the energy that will aggravate and perpetuate that thought. Guilt and anger are the twin ills of the amygdala, the seat of the superego and id.

Repeated exposure to guilt makes one guilt-sensitive. In this instance guilt becomes very painful and aggravates the behaviour that is desired to be controlled.

When someone makes you feel guilty, it can lead to masochism, causing you to seek out physical punishment. The person dishing out the physical punishment, such as whipping, caning, or beating with the fists is less at fault than the person who made you feel guilty. Also, guilt is more painful, distressing and destructive than physical punishment. Guilt can permanently damage the mind and behaviour, leaving the person helpless and hopeless. If someone making you feel guilty causes you to suicide, he should be up on a murder charge rather than pretend that he is innocent or even self-righteous. It is next to impossible to prove this type of crime in court, but the person committing it is just as much a criminal as the most brutal murderer.

Striving for Peace and Tolerance In the World One Person At A Time

The goal of peace and tolerance in the world, between nations, groups, and individuals, boils down to people feeling good about themselves leading to them feeling good about others. This is part of my belief as a Jew who also follows the Quaker religion. We must not punish people, especially the mentally ill, and especially retroactively. My sisters would like to castigate me in this way. Forgiveness is what peace is all about. People who want to punish others are hypocrites. I also had a principal, who used to punish in a particularly brutal way. We need less people like them if we are to have peace. They start war and violence, one person at a time.

Psychologists and mental health professionals, and I am one, tell us that the main cause of religious, racial, sexual, and intolerance of any kind is people having low self-esteem. This caused the Nazis, the Ku Klux Klan and indeed my principal who tried to murder me to behave the way they did. There are a number of therapies for the problem. Using any therapy and improving people's self-respect is against violence.

Violence is a matter of transgressing the rights of the individual. Physical violence is a matter of violating the right of a person to decide what is done with his body. Psychological violence is a matter of violating the person's right to his psychological dignity. Both forms of violence are bad. I believe in not answering violence with violence. Violence of any kind begets violence again. Trying to induce someone to feel guilty is another form of violence. My principal was a particularly bad transgressor of all forms of violence. He particularly liked guns, war and military service. He was a monster and would not put his own self in harm's way.

People with low self-esteem tend to try to overcome it by running others down. My sisters were like that and I am the target. My parents encouraged it.

The belief that the light of God shines in all people, including yourself not only promotes a good feeling in yourself and others, but is a major step toward promoting peace. It leads to us behaving in constructive ways for ourselves and others. The human condition is finite, but the light of God that shines in everyone is forever.

On examining the content of various teachers and principals such as the one who told me to kill myself, it appears that delusions of reference factored heavily into this idea and he may not be as bad as some of my writing makes him out to be. Unfortunately, these delusions of reference almost got me killed.

Some Thoughts On Courage

The dictionare defines courage as steadiness in enduring danger or pain. It consists of using will power to control the natural shrinking that we all feel in danger or pain situations. Will power is dependent on how much we want to do something, inhibited by limiting factors such as anxiety, meaning courage is dependent largely on how much we want to have it. Courage is a form of love and love is a form of courage. M. Scott Peck defined love as a will to extend oneself to promote the spiritual growth of someone. By spiritual, he meant the mind. Therefore, I define courage as a will to extend yourself to do something useful. Everyone has courage. We cannot live without it. Work, academics writing, and exercise are examples of this form of courage. As an example, I particularly mention Nilani Cohen. It is my position of being a PhD psychologist, specializing in anxiety reduction, that makes me a particular expert on courage. People who are skilled in anxiety reduction through relaxation can endure the pain of childbirth and the danger of battle.

In my theorizing, I have eliminated the scourge of cowardice the same way that Thomas Szasz has eliminated mental illness. He says there is no such thing as mental illness, only problems in living. He says that mental illness is a myth. I say that cowardice is a myth. It does not exist, only missed opportunities.

Also, I should mention the courage of Dr. Frank Sommers, who went into a dangerous combat zone in Kandahar, Afghanistan, to serve his country and help soldiers as well as the people of Afghanistan, and wound up enriching the lives of all his patients, as he does everyday.

Courageous is someone you like and cowardly is someone you don't like. We like one third of the people we meet, no matter what they do, we are indifferent to another third and dislike the last third. I was unfortunate to be born into a family consisting of the last third that dislike me. They wanted a male child, but soon found out that they wanted to send me back to where I came from because I had a normal temper. Incidentally, the dictionary defines coward as a mean, vile, worthless individual.

Consultation Report from George Foussias, MD FRCPC

Here is a report from Dr. George Foussias. I was referred to him by Dr. Jeff Daskalakis as part of an experiment in deep brain stimulation, which involves a surgical operation in two steps. Dr. Foussias and the neurosurgeons involved were reputed to be the best psychiatrists and neurosurgeons in the world. I believe it.

Thank you for referring Mr. Cohen for diagnostic assessment and recommendations with regards to negative symptoms. He was seen on June 18, 2013 and I also had the opportunity to review the past medical records.

Mr. Cohen is a 59 yr. Old gentleman, married since October 2011, with no kids, and supported financially by CPP. He is currently not employed and has not worked steadily since approximately 2002.

Mr. Cohen has a long history of schizophrenia dating back to approximately 1987, although it appears that he experienced a series of psychotic symptoms starting in his teenage years. At that time, symptoms included prominent auditory hallucinations, making derogatory comments, as well as various delusions including delusions of reference, persecutory delusions, grandiose delusions as well as delusions of thought control, mind reading, thought broadcasting, nihilism, and grandiosity. He has been treated with antipsychotic medications over the years including perphenazine, which he was being treated with for the longest period of time with doses up to 72 mg. Although it appears that the average dose was between 16 and 20 mg per day. He has also been tried on haloperidol and trifluoperazine. Chlorpromazine, and Nozinan. It appears that despite treatment with these medications that he has continued at the best of times to experience residual psychotic symptoms, although with improved irritability and anger that he experiences in response to the auditory hallucinations. More recently, he has been treated with risperidone currently at 2 mg bid, which has been somewhat helpful but with ongoing psychotic symptoms and hyperprolactinaemia with consequent sexual dysfunction. He has had a few admission to hospital including North York General Hospital at the age of 20 as well as two admissions to St. Michael's Hospital in 1987 and 1989. It appears that his admission in 1987 was in response to a suicide attempt where in response to voices he was hearing, he states that he jumped in front of the subway, but was not hit by the subway. He does not endorse any subsequent suicide attempts.

Mr. Cohen describes an ongoing history of psychotic symptoms including around made thoughts, made feelings, and made actions with particular influence from other people from his past and a sense that overall his behaviour is being controlled by others. He does not endorse any frank auditory hallucinations at the present time, although this appears to be largely in response to TMS treatments he had about 8 years ago. He does not endorse any delusions of grandiosity, religiosity, or referential delusions at the present time. He states that the severity of his psychotic symptoms fluctuate with some days and weeks where he feels good and other times when he becomes very angry and irritated in response to these symptoms. He also describes long-standing fluctuations in his mood with episodes of up to several weeks where he feels depressed and other times where he feels good. He describes reduction in his experience of pleasure, reduction in his sex drive, as well as feelings of guilt and hopelessness and feeling slowed psychomotorically. He states that his energy is good as is his appetite. He does describe difficulties with his attention and memory. He does not endorse any suicidal or homicidal ideation. With regards to his sleep, it appears that it is chronically erratic over the past four years, only sleeping a handful of hours early in the evening followed by being awake between midnight and 6 am and then subsequently sleeping again until 11 am. In addition, he describes some compulsive behaviour including frequent list making which he needs to do every two to three days as well a some vague reports of hoarding, although this was not flushed out in detail. He does not endorse any symptoms of generalized anxiety disorder or panic disorder nor any social anxiety. In addition, he does not endorse any history of mania.

With regard to negative symptoms, Mr. Cohen describes a prominent loss of will and motivation dating back to approximately 2002. He states at that time that he stopped working following the death of his father to take care of his elderly mother who had Alzheimer's disease and essentially was her full-time caregiver. She passed away in October, 2009, and he states that he continued to experience a drop in his motivation since that time. With regards to interests, he states that he has lost his enjoyment in activities, and one further examination, he seems to have a reduced range of both positive and negative emotional experiences, although does report some positive experiences and some negative experiences with restricted range. He describes the course of his day as consisting of spending much time with his wife, going outside for walks on a daily basis for between 30 and 60 minutes, at times swimming, going to appointments several times a week as well as going for walks on to buy a pop or go to a magazine shop where he browses through the table of contents of magazines that he is interested in, and at times buys one as well. Apart from his wife, his social network is quite restricted with only a recent friend that he is connected with and sees for coffee once to twice per week. He has two sisters who live in the area, one of whom he has no contact with and the second with whom he talks to infrequently on the phone. And does not look forward to speaking with her or to her visits. He does, however, state a series of goals for himself as well as attempts to achieve those goals. Of particular note is that over the last few years he has written several books and recently had one of his books published in December 2012. In addition, he does not spend much time sitting around or lying around or passively watching his time. When exploring his social network in further detail, he states that he does enjoy spending time with his wife, although at times feels lonely. He in addition describes enjoying some time with his new friend and that he is often the one that initiates phone calls and for them to meet.

Mr. Cohen's current medications consist of risperidone 2 mg bid and Effexor 300 mg qam. He has no known drug allergies.

Mr. Cohen's past medical history is significant for arthritis, tendonitis including in his elbow, shoulder, and biceps tendon, as well as degenerative disc disease in his neck and lower back pain. He does not endorse any history of surgeries nor any history of seizures, blackouts, or loss of consciousness. He does have ongoing hyperprolactinaemia.

He does not have a significant substance use history, does not smoke any cigarettes, or drink any alcohol.

Mr. Cohen does not have any formal legal history.

With regards to his personal history, Mr. Cohen completed high school, went on to do a degree in nursing, and worked as a personal support worker for several years. He subsequently completed a PhD in Health Sciences and Psychology in the late 90s and practiced for one year after which time he stopped to take care of his mother after his father died in December 2002.

His past occupational history is significant for a number of other odd jobs including working at a shoe store for a couple of months, working as a messenger for several months, and a very recent job for a month where his worked as a janitor but was fired because he could not keep up with the pace of the work and had injured himself which he attributes to physical pain and physical limitations that he experiences. He states that in addition to his wife and the new friend that he has made, he does not have any other significant friendships, although does have some acquaintances with people he is in touch with over email. With regards to future goals, he states that he is interested in continuing to write and trying to get his books published as well as a series of physical goals including swimming longer distances, rock climbing, and learning more about science, technology, medicine, and learning a trade that may be helpful for him getting work.

On mental status examination, Mr. Cohen was properly dressed and cooperative throughout the interview. He did not appear to be responding to internal stimuli. He exhibited a normal degree of eye contact. His speech was of normal rate, rhythm, and volume and spontaneous in nature with no evidence of poverty. His affect exhibited mild blunting, although with a full range and appropriately reactive. His thought form was coherent, goal directed and future oriented. He endorsed a series of long-standing delusions of reference, control, and thought insertion. He did not endorse any perceptual disturbances at the present time. He did not endorse any suicidal or homicidal ideation. His insight and judgement appeared appropriate. There did not appear to be any gross cognitive abnormalities with the exceptional of mild inattention with one error on serial 7s but appropriate ability to spell "world" backwards. He was oriented to time and place.

Impression

My impression is that this 59 year old gentleman with a long history of psychotic symptoms continues to meet diagnostic criteria for schizophrenia as well as some fluctuating depressive symptoms that over the last three week period have improved somewhat. It does appear, however, that at times he does meet criteria for major depressive episode. In addition, he does endorse negative symptoms, particularly around reduction in interests and motivation and social drive. Although one detailed questioning, it appears that there is a breadth of interests and goals that he is able to set for himself, although the range of his internal emotional experiences appears somewhat reduced. My overall assessment would be that his negative symptoms are in the mild to moderate range. There did not appear to be any acute safety concerns.

MultiAxial Diagnoses

Axis 1 Schizophrenia and possible major depressive episode versus schizoaffective disorder, depressive subtype.

Axis 2 Hyperprolactinaemia, arthritis, tendonitis, degenerative disk disease, and low back pain.

Recommendations

Given Mr. Cohen's past treatment history, it appears he has had a series of medication trials without any consistent evidence of remission of his positive symptoms. In light of this, he would be an appropriate candidate for a trial of clozapine which was introduced briefly to him during our assessment, although without much details around monitoring or side effects. Ultimately, it appears that some important contributors to his apparent negative symptoms and his self-reported loss of will and drive are likely connected to both his ongoing residual positive symptoms and depressive symptoms. In light of these other symptom domains, it is difficult to ascertain what the severity of his underlying primary negative symptoms is. For this reason, it would be appropriate to actively pursue treatment of these other symptom domains first with subsequent focus on negative symptoms after adequate resolution of his other difficulties.

In addition, he would likely benefit from engagement in group activities that may be available through your clinic and he was encouraged to enquire further about these.

I hope this will be of some assistance in your treatment of this gentleman.

Since medication helps my inferior gender identity, it is logical to conclude that my inferior gender identity and also masochism are part of schizophrenia and probably most that is bad about me is caused by schizophrenia.

Every one of my voices are things people have actually said to me. If I tell myself that these are not true, I either do no hear the voices of they lose their sting.

Having schizophrenia is like looking at life and reality from behind a prism. The prism distorts our perception of reality so that our actions are a rough guess at whether they are based on an accurate perception. Anyone, and everyone can have a distorted perception of reality. In fact if someone gets 98% on a test, his perception of reality is off by 2%. However, that type of misperception is nowhere near as distressing as schizophrenia.

Life Timeline

Years 1- 10 – very unhappy

Years 10- 12 – I realized I was very ill

Age 12 – first nervous breakdown

Ages 13 &14 – recovering from nervous breakdown

Age 15 – best year of life due to best mental health

ever Age 16 – bad due to starting schizophrenia

Age 17 – bad due to worsening schizophrenia

Age 18 – bad due to worsening schizophrenia and abusive school

Age 19 – good year with some letdowns

Age 20 – next nervous breakdown

Ages 21 – 24 – worked 16 hours per day at university

Age 25 – worked at JVS and recovered from generalized anxiety disorder

Age 25 – great time working at Fred Victor Mission

Age 26 – nursing school was enjoyable, but disappointing that cognitive deficit worsened and could not finish

Age 27 – worked for Comcare and St. John's Rehabilitation

Age 30 – started at Grace Hospital

Age 34 – major mental meltdown due to perphenazine stopping its good work

- worked for Young Canada shoes and The Messengers
- age 35 – worked for Gordon-Daly Grenadier and exercised for 2-3 hrs./day
- age 36 – worked at St. Francis mental health residence
- age 37 – 41 – Comcare
- ages 41 – 49 – Infogroup and PhD and cared for Diane
- ages 49 – 56 – cared for mother 24/7 with very little help
- age 58 – married Nilani, grow old along with me, the best is yet to be.

As another afterthought in this book, since I was 16, I have had the delusion that my thoughts, feelings, and behaviour were controlled by others. The doctor informed me that this is a delusion that is common in schizophrenia and that it is not possible for others to control one's thoughts, feelings, and behaviour. I am currently trying to rid this delusion with help from my medication. If I could rid this delusion, it would be a major step forward and a significant sign of growth. This delusion had previously been put in remission without my realizing it, with help from my miraculous response to perphenazine. This delusion is a big reason that schizophrenics have low self-esteem and is primarily a function of primitive parts of the brain, most notably the limbic system and its excess supply of dopamine. I was shocked to learn that it is not possible for one's thoughts, feelings, and behaviour to be controlled by others. The doctor who caused my schizophrenia suggested that not having opinions of one's own and not being independent is caused by not acknowledging thought of sex and aggression. That might be a psychoanalytic theory and I am not sure what the answer is. I want to research this problem more. It is probably related to the idea of emotional independence. Confidence and pride in oneself and feeling that one can handle anything that comes along is probably helpful.

In researching delusions with Google, it has been said that my insight is a step forward in ridding a delusion.

This delusion of mind control feels like being sent to jail for bad behaviour. I have had it since the day I was assaulted, approximately fourty-eight years ago, when I was about fifteen years and nine months old. It probably comes from the amygdala in the brain and seems to be related to guilt and anger and suspiciousness which are the bad things brought about by the amygdala and primitive parts of the brain, overactive in schizophrenics. It feels like jail, but originally I was sent to jail for a crime I did not commit and later felt I should go to jail for things I did. Both ideas are signs of severe illness. It was in trying to fight this delusion, and assisted by the psychiatrists idiotic therapy and suggestions that I became the worst violent. If I can develop a realistic regret, which does not include ridiculous guilt and my family shaming me for being a bad person, that would be a good outcome. I have long felt that I deserved to be in this jail, even before my disease caused inappropriate aggression. That is probably part of my disease. I hope to be released from this jail before I die, anyway and the doctor feels that a higher dose of my paliperidone injection would help. Medication given by injection works better than medication given by mouth, perhaps because it gets absorbed better. I have found it very helpful. If I could get over the delusions of mind control in terms of thoughts and feelings, it would be the ultimate in bliss.

It has also been suggested by the people, family and teachers who think I am the ultimate in evil, Adolf Hitler that I should undergo capital punishment and torture. The people suggesting these treatments are the evil ones even for suggesting that I am immature and inferior for any ridiculous reasons they can find that agree with their hatred of me. These ideas are absurd and barbaric and belong in the garbage. Also, the non-constructive ideas of family, teachers, and the former psychiatrist fuel my problems and make violence more likely. Guilt is belief that you have done something wrong and punishes. Shame is belief that you are a bad person and punishes even more and is very destructive. Also, shame is not indicative that you really are a bad person. I have certain family members who say that they never do anything wrong and that lack of guilt shows goodness. This is the type of self-righteousness of psychopaths and sociopaths and if it were true, Paul Bernardo, O.J. Simpson and Adolf Hitler would be the most virtuous people ever, along with these teachers and family members.

Also, it has been suggested that people become mentally ill because they do not face reality. This is not true because the unreality of delusions and hallucinations are so horrible that no one would choose. These delusions such as delusions of guilt are from primitive centres of the brain, so far removed from our lofty, noble side.

Speaking of our lofty, noble side, altruistic ideas of wanting to help people aside from helping our own problems are likely dependent on not having problems and pain ourselves. If I had not had a tough life, I would not be in so much pain. So thumbs down to the above-mentioned jerks.

Albert Schweitzer and Ernest Hemingway were true men who suffered from depression and guilt that only occurs in adults and were very good people.

The very low esteem that my family held me in is very opposite to the positive spin and high esteem I held loved ones like Nilani and Diane in and is a sign of hatred, although we all got along well enough to live together and do things together. Living with my parents was mutually beneficial and should not be looked down on like my family and others have. Even my parents started to raise their opinion of me partly due to finally realizing I was not as bad as some made me out to be and realizing what I had been through. In the few times that my family has said good things about me, it can be described as "they know the words, but not the music." Also, in coping with the biochemical imbalance without medication in my teens, it could be compared to the labours of Hercules, as were some of the feats of physical courage that I did.

I am the first one to say that the ideas of schizophrenia are not adult and constructive. Maybe someday, I will be something of the real man I was when I was fifteen. Take the best and leave the rest.

Maturity is associated with many characteristics, but the definition of a mature person as elaborated on by a neuropsychiatrist that I talked to and was an expert is one who can take responsibility for his actions. This is primarily a function of conscience. That is one of the reasons why conscience-related depression only occurs in adults. I show this conscience, even though it does not serve anyone, including myself, well. My relatives do not. They know the words, but not the music, characteristic of sociopaths. This lack of responsibility caused Adolf Hitler to flee at the Munich beer hall. It tends to be associated with cowardice. Unfortunately, the excessive conscience of schizophrenia is not good for anybody and is non-constructive. Constructiveness correlates with maturity and my principal and doctor who just laugh off their misdeeds are very puerile, and did enormous damage. Damaging even one person in this way is most egregious. Maturity when properly expressed correlates with goodness, constructiveness and good mental health. Something good for your mental health is good for everyone and the converse is true for something bad for your mental health. Just because I have never known anything but mental illness does not mean that I am immature or bad. Also, courage results from self-control and is another function of conscience.

My family members all say that my schizophrenia is genetic. They mockingly call me a GI, genetically inferior, a phrase used by many bigots and Adolf Hitler used it to justify his extermination policy. If it was solely genetic, it would have shown up much earlier and without needing me to be assaulted as I was. My family is not constructive and are full of hatred. The doctor who caused my schizophrenia was an enormous hypocrite and used to contradict himself often. He was essentially a member of the family.

www.ingramcontent.com/pod-product-compliance
Lightning Source LLC
Chambersburg PA
CBHW060504030426
42337CB00015B/1738